BIMSTEC TRADE FACILITATION STRATEGIC FRAMEWORK 2030

DECEMBER 2022

BIMSTEC

ADB

© 2022 Asian Development Bank
6 ADB Avenue, Mandaluyong City, 1550 Metro Manila, Philippines
Tel +63 2 8632 4444; Fax +63 2 8636 2444
www.adb.org

Some rights reserved. Published in 2022.

ISBN 978-92-9269-904-8 (print); 978-92-9269-905-5 electronic); 978-92-9269-906-2 (ebook)
Publication Stock No. TCS220542-2
DOI: http://dx.doi.org/10.22617/TCS220542-2

The views expressed in this publication are those of the authors and do not necessarily reflect the views and policies of the Asian Development Bank (ADB) or its Board of Governors or the governments they represent.

ADB does not guarantee the accuracy of the data included in this publication and accepts no responsibility for any consequence of their use. The mention of specific companies or products of manufacturers does not imply that they are endorsed or recommended by ADB in preference to others of a similar nature that are not mentioned.

By making any designation of or reference to a particular territory or geographic area, or by using the term "country" in this document, ADB does not intend to make any judgments as to the legal or other status of any territory or area.

Please contact pubsmarketing@adb.org if you have questions or comments with respect to content, or if you wish to obtain copyright permission for your intended use that does not fall within these terms, or for permission to use the ADB logo.

Corrigenda to ADB publications may be found at http://www.adb.org/publications/corrigenda.

Notes:
In this publication, "$" refers to United States dollars.

The main work for the preparation of this report was undertaken in 2020 and 2021, while trade and trade facilitation activities were substantially curtailed in the BIMSTEC countries due to the pandemic. Periodic updates were made in 2022 based on inputs from the BIMSTEC member states. However, since updated data was not consistently available, it is recognized that some sections may not necessarily reflect the most current status of trade facilitation in the member states.

Cover design by Edith Creus.

CONTENTS

TABLES, FIGURES, AND BOX

Box

FOREWORD

This year marks the 25th anniversary of the establishment of the Bay of Bengal Initiative for Multi-Sectoral Technical and Economic Cooperation (BIMSTEC), which was established on 6 June 1997 with the signing of the Bangkok Declaration. The founding leaders of BIMSTEC envisioned the promotion of free trade and increased cross-border investment which led to underscoring trade and investment as one of the key sectors of cooperation.

One of the primary objectives of the establishment of BIMSTEC was to promote intra-regional trade and investment in the Bay of Bengal region. Remaining faithful to this objective, BIMSTEC concluded the Framework Agreement on the BIMSTEC Free Trade Area in 2004. The Framework Agreement encouraged establishment of effective trade and investment facilitating measures, including simplification of customs procedures, and development of mutual recognition arrangements, among others. The Permanent Secretariat of BIMSTEC recognizes the importance of developing a long-term strategic framework for the sector identifying the specific requirements to enhance trade facilitation activities in the region under the framework of BIMSTEC.

The BIMSTEC Trade Facilitation Strategic Framework 2030, which has been conducted by the Asian Development Bank (ADB), is an important endeavor to advance trade facilitation among member states. It highlights the existing challenges of free trade among member states and identifies strategies to combat the challenges to achieve specific goals. This Strategic Framework suggests a structured pathway approach to enhancing the regional trade facilitation environment over the coming decade.

One of the core challenges to creating a regional trade facilitation framework has been the difference in members' conditions and their capacities to foster trade facilitation. While some member states have significantly developed their trade facilitation arrangement, other member states are yet to perform many activities required. Keeping this divergence and geographic limitations, the BIMSTEC Trade Facilitation Strategic Framework 2030 provides general recommendations for the region at large.

This framework has precisely outlined various soft infrastructure, hard infrastructure, and other cooperation, and capacity-building strategies. It has also identified that the implementation of the BIMSTEC Trade Facilitation Strategy will be guided by seven principles namely, (i) country ownership, (ii) results-orientation combined with pragmatism, (iii) flexibility and responsiveness to country needs, (iv) reform and modernization, (v) active participation and involvement of the private sector, (iv)partnerships with development partners, and (vii) mutual cooperation. The study report also recommends that the implementation of the Trade Facilitation Strategy would be funded from the internal resources of the BIMSTEC member states, as well as from the external resources of bilateral and multilateral development partners of the member states.

With the publication of the BIMSTEC Trade Facilitation Strategic Framework 2030, I wish to convey my warm thanks to ADB for its dedication and support in successfully conducting this study. I also thank all BIMSTEC member states, in particular Bangladesh, the lead country for trade, investment and development, for their support and cooperation in successfully completing the BIMSTEC Trade Facilitation Strategic Framework 2030.

I strongly believe that the BIMSTEC Trade Facilitation Strategic Framework 2030 will be an effective guiding tool for all member states in achieving their goals towards increased trade facilitation in the region.

Tenzin Lekphell
Secretary General
BIMSTEC

PREFACE

Trade has been a key area of cooperation since the inception of the Bay of Bengal Initiative for Multi-Sectoral Technical and Economic Cooperation (BIMSTEC), and expanding trade has been a cornerstone of BIMSTEC's efforts to deepen economic cooperation among member states. To expand trade, BIMSTEC is developing a free trade area and supporting trade facilitation initiatives aimed at eliminating or minimizing nontariff barriers.

Considerable progress on trade facilitation has been made across the region in recent years, but national performances in this area remain below most developed countries and market leaders. The current state of trade facilitation and the presence and impact of the nontariff barriers also varies significantly between BIMSTEC member states. These differences need to be taken into account in a common framework approach, which applies to all member states.

Hence, the BIMSTEC Trade Facilitation Strategic Framework 2030 has been developed to tackle nontariff barriers by providing a structured pathway to enhance the BIMSTEC region's trade facilitation environment. It is based on a standard strategic planning structure that sets out BIMSTEC's trade facilitation vision, how this is to be achieved, methods to be adopted, and the goals to be met through investment in hard and soft infrastructure, capacity building, and cooperation. While recognizing the trade facilitation arrangements that BIMSTEC member states have signed with other regional groupings and initiatives, this strategic framework responds to the specific trade facilitation needs of BIMSTEC member states and the supportive role it can play in achieving the goal of setting up a free trade area. Its comprehensive scope combines strategic and action planning to help enable its early implementation.

The intraregional and external trade of BIMSTEC member states has been disrupted by COVID-19. Thus, progress in implementing more advanced trade facilitation techniques has been severely constrained. That said, the temporary downturn in trade volume is also an opportunity—a window of change, so to speak—to embrace new approaches and technologies as the economies of BIMSTEC member states recover from the pandemic and discussions make progress on creating a free trade area.

Although BIMSTEC member states are facing challenging economic times, the resumption of trade growth will be critical for a return to stability. And because of this, increasing trade and enhancing trade facilitation are BIMSTEC priorities. To this end, the strategic framework shows how improvements in trade facilitation processes and procedures can be strengthened to support the implementation of BIMSTEC free trade area and ensure the region remains competitive in both regional and global trade.

ADB is pleased to support BIMSTEC in preparing this important report. I would like to acknowledge the extensive efforts of the study team from the Regional Cooperation and Operations Coordination Division, South Asia Department. I would also like to thank officials in the BIMSTEC Secretariat and member states, staff from ADB resident missions, the Southeast Asia Department, the Department of Communications, and the Regional Cooperation and Integration Thematic Group, and other stakeholders for providing substantial comments to improve the report. All their contributions are gratefully acknowledged.

K. Yokoyama

Kenichi Yokoyama
Director General
South Asia Department
Asian Development Bank

ABBREVIATIONS

ADB	Asian Development Bank
AEO	Authorized economic operator
AFTA	ASEAN Free Trade Area
APEC	Asia-Pacific Economic Cooperation
ASEAN	Association of Southeast Asian Nations
ASYCUDA	Automated System for Customs Data
BACS	Bhutan Automated Customs System
BIMSTEC	Bay of Bengal Initiative for Multi-Sectoral Technical and Economic Cooperation
CBIC	Central Board of Indirect Taxes and Customs
CFS	Container freight station
COVID-19	Coronavirus disease
EU	European Union
FTA	Free Trade Agreement
GMS	Greater Mekong Subregion
GVC	Global value chain
ICD	Inland clearance/container depot
ICEGATE	Indian Customs Electronic Gateway
ICES	Indian Customs Electronic Data Exchange System
ICP	integrated check post
ICT	Information and communication technology
IFI	International financial institution
LPI	Logistics Performance Index
MRA	Mutual recognition agreement
MSMEs	Micro, small, and medium-sized enterprises
NAFTA	North American Free Trade Agreement
NBR	National Board of Revenue
NSW	National single window
NTB	Nontariff barrier
NTTFC	National Trade and Transport Facilitation Committee
OECD	Organisation for Economic Co-operation and Development
PCS	Port community system
PPP	Public-Private Partnership
PRC	People's Republic of China
RAMIS	Revenue Administration and Management Information System
RCEP	Regional Comprehensive Economic Partnership
RKC	Revised Kyoto Convention on the Simplification and Harmonization of Customs
SAARC	South Asian Association for Regional Cooperation

SAFE	Standards to Secure and Facilitate Trade
SAFTA	South Asia Free Trade Area
SASEC	South Asia Subregional Economic Cooperation
SITPRO	Simplification and Harmonization of Trade Procedures
SWIFT	Single Window Interface for Facilitating Trade
SMEs	Small and medium enterprises
TFA	Trade Facilitation Agreement
UNECE	United Nations Economic Commission for Europe
UNESCAP	United Nations Economic and Social Commission for Asia and the Pacific
US	United States
USAID	United States Agency for International Development
WCO	World Customs Organization
WTO	World Trade Organization

EXECUTIVE SUMMARY

Introduction and Background

One of the core functions of the Bay of Bengal Initiative for Multi-Sectoral Technical and Economic Cooperation (BIMSTEC) is promoting free trade and increasing cross-border investments. Trade was identified as one of the six sectors of BIMSTEC cooperation at the grouping's inception in 1997 in recognition of the important role trade can play in national and regional economic growth. The expansion of intraregional trade between member states can become the cornerstone of their economic cooperation.

BIMSTEC has adopted a twin approach in tackling regional trade constraints. The BIMSTEC Free Trade Area initiative has been specifically planned to help eliminate or minimize the tariff barriers that adversely affect intraregional trade, whereas the parallel trade facilitation program is designed to tackle the nontariff barriers (NTBs) affecting trade in general. The BIMSTEC Trade Facilitation Strategic Framework 2030 provides a structured pathway approach for enhancing the environment for trade facilitation until 2030. The main constraints to improving trade facilitation have been the NTBs that have resulted in higher costs for the trading communities in the member states.

The trade facilitation environment differs significantly among BIMSTEC member countries. Various international trade facilitation performance indicators suggest India and Thailand have the most advanced facilitation environment in the region, followed by Bangladesh, Myanmar, and Sri Lanka. Landlocked Bhutan and Nepal are seen as having the least advanced trade facilitation environment at this stage. These differences need to be acknowledged within a common framework approach, whereby proposed strategies apply to all member states to a greater or lesser extent, but with national variations and situations being also taken into account. Despite significant progress in trade facilitation being made in the region over the last decade, national trade facilitation environments remain substantially below those of most developed countries and the market leaders in adjacent regions.

The coronavirus disease (COVID-19) has had a significant impact on the BIMSTEC region. The pandemic has resulted in a temporary downturn in trade and an increased reliance on automated systems ("process distancing") for customs clearances in some member states. Although the pandemic is expected to continue affecting the Strategic Framework's implementation in the short- to medium-term, it also offers a "window of change" opportunity to embrace new approaches and technologies to enhance performance in an evolving trade environment.

Expanding the Scope of Trade Facilitation

The most common definition of trade facilitation is the streamlining of customs and border procedures to enable imports and exports to flow more rapidly across borders. Trade facilitation in the BIMSTEC region under the various initiatives adopted by international financial institutions (IFIs) and member state governments since 2000 has tended to concentrate on modernizing border infrastructure, advancing automated customs processing systems, and establishing customs cooperation mechanisms.

Because of the successful implementation of trade facilitation in these three areas in recent years, these institutions have gradually broadened their assistance to include other border agencies, including those responsible for sanitary, phytosanitary, and trading standards. They have also addressed the need for more so-called behind-the-border reforms in response to the overall need to reduce trade costs. This suggests a gradual change of emphasis from trade facilitation predominantly being driven by the needs of border authorities to one that is more orientated toward satisfying the growing demands of the wider trading community.

The Asia-Pacific Economic Cooperation has adopted an even broader interpretation of trade facilitation, called the "new generation." This approach reinforces the change from the physical movement of goods through borders to the demands created by changes in the logistics environment, whereby border transit merely represents an individual link within the overall international logistics chain. This more advanced interpretation is focused on improving the time, cost, and reliability of trade facilitation activities.

Against this backdrop, the scope of BIMSTEC trade facilitation needs to be broader than its traditional approach when creating a strategic framework for the future. Core challenges that require addressing include improved compliance, the needs of both border control agencies and the wider trading community (stakeholders) regarding investments in hard and soft infrastructure, enhanced processing approaches to be able to increase the use of automated technologies, additional behind-the-border facilities and procedures, and the enabling of member states to use more advanced trading and logistical applications.

Free Trade Agreements

In planning framework strategies to tackle NTBs, it is important to be mindful of parallel actions to address tariff barriers. These tariff restraints principally affect trade already taking place within the region. The unknown is the extent to which tariff barriers are constraining trade that might otherwise have taken place and, alternatively, what the impact on generating additional trade would be if such tariff barriers were eliminated—in effect, the potential to translate latent trade demand into physical demand.

An evaluation of regional free trade areas—BIMSTEC, the South Asian Association for Regional Cooperation (SAARC), and the Association of Southeast Asian Nations (ASEAN)—and bilateral free trade agreements between BIMSTEC member states confirms that the demand is there to forge both regional and bilateral free trade agreements, as indicated by those currently being proposed and negotiated. The pathway to implementation is, however, complex and time-consuming, often resulting in extended lead times from initial agreement to final enactment. A noticeable trend in recent years has been the gradual move away from globalism toward protectionism. This is most apparent in the trade relations between the United States and the People's Republic of China, the renegotiation of the North American Free Trade Agreement, trade friction between the US and the European Union, and Brexit. These are nevertheless merely symptomatic of concerns over the "fairness" of international trade. This negative trend suggests that regional free trade agreements could become more difficult to negotiate quickly, as countries seek to balance their national and regional interests.

The successful implementation of regional and bilateral free trade agreements in reducing tariff barriers will make tackling NTBs all the more important. Such trade agreements lower tariff barriers and the negative impact of NTBs then become even more apparent, thus, resolving these will be critical for realizing the benefits to be gained from these agreements. The goal of increasing trade implicit in a BIMSTEC Free Trade Area agreement can only be fully realized through enhanced trade facilitation addressing NTBs present in the region.

Trade Facilitation Issues in the BIMSTEC Region

In preparing the strategic framework, it was important to identify current constraints to trade facilitation in the region. These largely emanate from the development status of member states and the specific constraints present in each member country. Inevitably, there are significant differences in both the status of national trade facilitation environments and the nature and impact of the challenges faced by individual member states. The strategic framework seeks to cover common concerns wherever possible, while acknowledging their relevance will vary nationally, given their individual situations.

The most pressing issue regarding trade currently is the adverse impact of COVID-19. All BIMSTEC countries had cases and took various mitigation measures, including lockdowns and border closures, to contain the spread of the disease. While vaccine programs were gradually rolled out in 2021, some forms of remedial restrictions against new strains are likely to remain well into 2022 and possibly into 2023. It is unlikely vaccine programs will be sufficiently widespread to provide the necessary level of international herd immunity to reduce infection risks to a level that will enable a full return to the pre-pandemic trading activity in the short-term. Many member states have lifted many of the restrictions but remain ready to reimpose them if new more serious strains arise.

In this context, it is important to separate the impact of COVID-19 restrictions on trade and those on trade facilitation. A common factor between the two has been the closure of state and national borders that have highlighted any potential trade facilitation weaknesses. International trade will continue to be severely constrained by such closures, not only in BIMSTEC countries but also in their main trading partners. Freight movements through seaports were initially less affected by COVID-19 than airfreight; the latter being hit by cuts in passenger flights on which most airfreight is carried. The combination of port closures and port congestion during 2021 and early 2022 has resulted in international sea freight rates, at the time of writing, being close to all-time highs and space availability continues to be limited, leading to supply shortages and disruptions in global value chains (GVCs).

Trade in all BIMSTEC countries fell significantly in 2020. World trade was already falling in 2019 due to trade disputes among major trading countries. Data from the World Trade Organization (WTO) showed global merchandise trade contracted by 5.3% in 2020, principally due to the COVID-19 pandemic; the WTO projected a rebound to 8.0% growth in 2021. Other forecasts suggest this growth will fall to 4.0% in 2022—still below the level of global merchandise trade before the pandemic.[*] After those projections were made in March 2021, the pandemic worsened in both developed and developing countries, suggesting appreciable downside risks to the forecasts. The resurgence of the Omicron variant, the lifting of fiscal support mechanisms applied to combat the pandemic, high commodity prices, and the Russian invasion of Ukraine have all combined to create inflationary pressures suggesting that 2022 trade growth is likely to be constrained.

The pandemic has negatively affected progress in modernizing trade facilitation, but with the reduction in overall trade volumes, many of the existing constraints will hopefully gradually be resolved. In some cases, the need for remedial action to tackle these problems has already encouraged more advanced approaches to be used and these are included in the Strategic Framework. The pandemic and its aftermath may have offered increased opportunities for change during a period of lower demand for services. Indeed, this situation may be a rare opportunity to instigate transformations within the trade facilitation environment while temporarily operating under less pressure.

Soft Infrastructure

The priority in advancing the BIMSTEC trade facilitation environment under the "new generation" concept is to reduce the time and cost of border transactions. Enhancing the trade facilitation performance of border agencies will only be possible through procedural changes, supported by investments in hard (physical) infrastructure, be they at a land border, seaport, airport, inland clearance depot, container freight station, or land port. Ample evidence exists to suggest that investments in hard infrastructure at borders in isolation often fail to generate the anticipated trade facilitation benefits unless these investments are reinforced by parallel improvements in clearance performance.

Modern border processing is designed around the concept of minimizing the interface between customs and other government agencies and the wider trading community, including their clearing agents. The key objective is to promote "process distancing" with clearance activities eventually being predominantly online, thereby reducing the need for direct interfacing. The following are considered to be the main trade facilitation issues in the BIMSTEC region that need to be addressed in the Strategic Framework and applied to a greater or lesser extent to all BIMSTEC countries:

- **Direct interface between border authorities and brokers.** Current methodologies still require high levels of face-to-face contact between customs and traders' representatives for handing over hard-copy documentation and during inspection and examination routines;
- **Automation levels.** Despite increased investment in automated systems, some member states' border authorities continue to rely on manual processing and physical signatures and use information technology systems for recording transactions rather than automated processing. Introducing national single windows remains problematic due to the lower levels of automation used by some border agencies and the institutional difficulties in integrating all the parties into this communal application;

---

[*]   World Trade Organization. WTO Stats Dashboard. https://stats.wto.org/dashboard/merchandise_en.html.

- **Rationalizing clearance documentation.** The main documentation required for import and export clearances has been reduced, but not yet to the levels present in developed countries—and despite automation, original documents, manual signatures, and large numbers of copies are often still required;
- **Limited use of risk management and numbers of approved economic operators.** Inspection and examination levels remain high in most member states despite the widespread introduction of risk management and the adoption of channeling techniques. There remain too few approved economic operators and risk management–supporting post-clearance audits;
- **Lack of pre-arrival processing and application of advanced rulings.** Border authorities continue to rely on commencing the processing of consignments only after the physical arrival of goods at borders, rather than starting the process in advance provided the necessary documentation is available. The application of advanced rulings designed to eliminate classification and valuation disputes when clearing imports remains limited in some countries;
- **Compliance with international trade facilitation agreements.** Member states are at differing stages in the ratification and implementation of the WTO's Trade Facilitation Agreement, the Revised Kyoto Convention, and the Standards to Secure and Facilitate Trade (SAFE) Framework of the World Customs Organization (WCO), all of which are designed for the adoption of international best practices;
- **Limited use of inland transit systems.** Most cargoes continue to be cleared at points of entry rather than close to points of final delivery, due to expensive transit control systems and incidence of almost "double clearance" procedures on transit cargo;
- **Poor institutional cooperation.** Border agencies often operate in isolation, focusing on their individual responsibilities, rather than being part of a cohesive clearance team. Cooperation and coordination between authorities on either side of a border or between ministries in adjacent countries can often be limited;
- **Outdated customs legislation.** Because trade facilitation needs to respond to changes in trade demands, dated customs legislation can inhibit the comprehensive use of automated processing and the introduction of advanced processing techniques;
- **Lack of mutual recognition agreements.** Certain imported products, such as foodstuffs and electricals, often require tests to be undertaken post-arrival due to the absence of mutual recognition agreements between authorities in the respective exporting and importing countries; and
- **Limited performance monitoring.** The low use or absence of monitoring tools, such as time-release studies, makes it difficult for stakeholders to measure whether performance is improving as a result of changes in processing, investment, and capacity building.

Hard Infrastructure

Resolving soft infrastructure constraints is critical for enhancing trade facilitation, but this needs to be supported by investment in complementary hard infrastructure—the facilities where the processes and procedures are physically conducted. The extent of this infrastructure can have a direct impact on the efficiency of border and inland clearance of both import and export trade. Developing infrastructure by governments and under regional programs, such as Asian Development Bank's Greater Mekong Subregion and the South Asia Subregional Economic Cooperation initiatives and World Bank programs, are generally project-based. Progress is defined by the planning or completion of specific physical infrastructure, with national or strategic plans also identifying projects that can potentially enhance the trade facilitation environment directly or indirectly. A BIMSTEC trade facilitation initiative would be expected to adopt a similar approach. The following highlights the types of infrastructure required and likely constraints in their provision:

- **Need for additional border facilities.** The important investments in land border infrastructure since 2000 have not always been reflected in enhanced transit times; this is sometimes due to poor ergonomics and other associated design concerns. Many secondary borders remain congested as they await funding for their modernization.
- **Demand for more inland container and clearance depots.** Most imports continue to clear at the points of entry rather than near their final destination due to a lack of approved clearance facilities in inland areas with concentrated import/export demand. This results in additional transport costs and longer turnaround times at borders. The shortage of such facilities risks increasing cargo "dwell" times and congestion, particularly at the major seaports.
- **Land port expansion.** Those facilities located adjacent to borders often merely move the point of congestion from the border control zone to a few kilometers inland without expediting overall transit times. Some BIMSTEC countries also levy a charge to use these land ports without providing any additional added-value services.
- **Shortage of container freight stations.** This is often the case outside seaport areas and is impeding the efficient handling of less-than-containerload cargoes, resulting in delayed clearances of consolidation traffic, thereby adding to the congestion in seaport container terminals.
- **Insufficient numbers of test laboratories.** Products arriving at land and sea borders requiring test certificates often need samples to be sent off to distant inland laboratories for testing, thus causing clearance delays. This can even result in the loss of merchandise, especially of perishable products.

Changes in Trade Logistics

The application of modern or advanced logistics in most BIMSTEC countries lags behind global standards. This is cited as a likely cause for the relatively poor performance of most of these countries in the World Bank's Logistics Performance Index. External pressures will result in changes in the way international trade is conducted, and it is critical that trade facilitation in the BIMSTEC region be capable of responding positively to these adjustments to avoid the creation of new NTBs. The following subjects relate to enhanced trade logistics:

- **Global value chain risks.** Clearance delays at borders can often compromise the ability of member states to attract GVC traffic due to the reliability risks adversely impacting supply chains and production line manufacturing;
- **Adaptability of trade facilitation to advanced logistical concepts.** Innovative logistical approaches practiced by stakeholders, such as vendor-managed inventory, e-commerce, just-in-time, and the application of new trading terms, are not always compatible with traditional border processing approaches and can meet the evolving demands of stakeholders; and
- **Constraints in linking national single windows to port community systems.** Where these two information technology (IT) systems exist, there is often no direct online interface between them. Due to this caveat, the tracking and tracing capability of the port community system are compromised due to the lack of data on the clearance status of shipments, resulting in delayed collections that then increase congestion risks.

Institution and Capacity Building

The trade facilitation demands of the global trading community over the next 10 years will change significantly, as will how border agencies respond to these changes. This will require the introduction of, or a more widespread application of, advanced processing and procedures, supported by even higher levels of automation. The traditional roles and working practices of customs officers and other border officials will also likely change markedly. The nature of this adjustment is difficult to predict, but examining the experiences of those countries with the most advanced trade facilitation environments provides clues. New approaches to processing and procedures will require institutional- and capacity-building programs to implement them. This will involve not only technical training but also changes in mindsets and trust, which will inevitably be more difficult to achieve at remoter land border posts and dry ports. The following are the main constraints relating to institution and capacity building:

- **Duplication of processing when automated and manual systems operate in parallel.** The main reason for this practice is that border officials have not always fully bought into these systems. This lack of trust means they often revert to manual processing with which they are more familiar and using the automated system as a transaction recording application rather than as a processing tool.
- **Insufficient skills upgrading.** Changes in trade facilitation require new skill sets and upskilling, but border authorities often have limited training programs and can suffer skills losses from high staff turnover and the adoption of personnel rotation regimes.
- **Shortage of experienced information technology personnel.** Border agencies find it difficult to attract and retain quality personnel to maintain and advance increasingly sophisticated IT applications due to the continued reliance on government pay scales. High IT staff turnover is a particular problem because of the intense competition from the private sector.
- **Limited cooperation between authorities in member states.** The status of trade facilitation varies significantly among BIMSTEC countries. Those with the most advanced trade facilitation environments have no established mechanism to assist the less advanced ones that continue to rely on external training and assistance programs.

Structure and Content of the Strategic Framework

While various structures can be used for the strategic framework, its contents must be compatible with the trade facilitation strategies that member states have already endorsed as members of other regional groupings. South Asia Subregional Economic Cooperation (SASEC) has the closest membership to BIMSTEC, with Thailand being the only non-member. SAARC does not include two BIMSTEC members: Myanmar and Thailand, while ASEAN, the Ayeyawady-Chao Phraya-Mekong Economic Cooperation Strategy, and the Greater Mekong Subregion (GMS) each only have two BIMSTEC members. This suggests compatibility with the current SASEC trade facilitation strategies is probably the most important, while also taking Thailand's situation into account.

Differentiating the strategic framework from these regional initiatives can be achieved through content rather than having a different structure. The proposed structure for this framework incorporates some structural elements from these regional initiatives, as the following shows:

- Overarching vision statement—links the framework to BIMSTEC's overall strategic vision, thereby providing *regional context*;

- Vision statement—defines *what* the framework is expected to accomplish and *why*;
- Mission statement—identifies *how* the vision will be achieved and is action-based;
- Strategic statement—indicates *the methods* to fulfill the framework's mission;
- Goal—identifies what needs *to be accomplished* to realize the strategic framework and what needs to be done to be able to monitor progress being achieved;
- Components—defines *the areas* to be addressed under the framework; and
- Subcomponent strategies and goals—identifies how each subcomponent will need to be addressed to make progress in achieving the various subcomponent goals leading to *achieving the overall goal.*

Supporting cross-cutting components needs to be included in the strategic framework. These components include the guiding principles applied in formulating the framework, mobilizing resources to implement the framework, monitoring mechanisms to identify progress being made in achieving the framework's goals, and the cooperation and institutional mechanisms required to manage the initiative.

The core constituent is achieving the overall framework goal through proposals for each of the components that represent the essential challenges to be addressed. Each of these components identifies specific constraints relevant to that particular component, followed by a strategy identifying pathways toward its resolution, and finally suggests achievable goals towards resolving the constraint. These component-level goals can also be used to monitor progress in the framework's implementation.

Priorities have not generally been included because the trade facilitation environments of member states are at differing stages of progress in their development. Even so, a common priority is to reduce the time and cost of border transactions, be they at a land border, seaport, airport, or inland clearance depot. Investments in a combination of soft and hard infrastructure, in particular, will be needed to achieve this goal.

The constraints, strategies, and goals at the component level addressed in the strategic framework are:

Soft Infrastructure

- Increased remote processing and clearances

  Strategy: BIMSTEC will encourage member states to progressively increase the application of online processing and e-clearances, particularly at land, maritime, and aviation borders, and inland clearance depots.

  Goal: Most import and export clearances in member states should be processed by automated systems, and confirmation of their clearance and release posted online to traders or their agents, thereby limiting the need for face-to-face contact.

- Automation

  Strategy: BIMSTEC will encourage border agencies in member states to maximize the submission and processing of import, export, and transit declarations using automated systems and the clearance of shipments whenever possible without the need for manual intervention, other than in the case of shipments requiring inspection or examination.

BIMSTEC will encourage all the other main border agencies to invest in the application of automated processing systems and member states to continue planning, improving, and expanding national single windows and trade information portals.

Goals: Automated processing should become the norm from e-filing of declarations through to the payment of duties and final release, thereby minimizing manual interventions. All member states should have fully operational national single windows linking all relevant border agencies operational by 2030 and comprehensive trade information portals by 2025.

- Rationalizing documentation

Strategy: BIMSTEC will encourage member states to reduce the number of original documents and copies required for import, export, or transit declarations. Clearance should increasingly become based on e-submissions rather than relying on the submission of original documents at the time of e-filing. BIMSTEC will also encourage the use of international format documentation wherever possible.

Goal: A reduction in documentary requirements by customs to less than six core import or export documents to enable a clearance by 2025 (excluding those required by other border agencies). Submission of original documentation should not be mandatory at the time of e-filing and the number of copy documents should be gradually reduced to less than five supporting copies by 2030.

- Application of advanced procedures

Strategy: BIMSTEC will encourage member states to reduce overall physical inspection and examination levels through the widespread application of risk management and the approval of more authorized economic operators or "trusted traders." This will expedite border clearances even though it may require increased post-clearance auditing to ensure compliance.

BIMSTEC will encourage member states to introduce pre-arrival processing, provided that the necessary supporting data is available in advance and that the advanced ruling services should become more widely accessible.

Goal: By applying risk management and authorized economic operator programs, the percentage of green channel shipments should gradually increase and physical examination levels decrease, compared to 2020 levels. Post-audit capabilities should be expanded by training more specialist units, pre-arrival processing should be permitted in all member states by 2025, and advanced-ruling capacities expanded to meet potential future demand.

- Compliance with international agreements and conventions

Strategy: BIMSTEC will encourage member states to implement the articles and recommendations contained in the Trade Facilitation Agreement, the Revised Kyoto Convention, and the SAFE Framework, irrespective of whether they have been ratified by the member state or not.

Goals: Based on the TFA implementation categories for developing countries (Category A will implement within 1 year; Category B will implement after a transitional period; and Category C will implement after a transitional period but assistance and support for capacity building will be required).

India, Thailand	TFA: all Category B/C to A by the end of 2024
Bangladesh, Sri Lanka	TFA: all Category C to A or B by the end of 2023 and all Category B to A by the end of 2026
Myanmar, Nepal, Bhutan	TFA: 20% Category A, 40% Category B, 40% Category C by the end of 2023, 40% Category A and 40% Category B and only 20% Category C by the end of 2026

- Transit systems

Strategies: BIMSTEC will encourage member states to adopt the more widespread application of transit procedures, thereby reducing the proportion of imports needing to be fully cleared at the point of entry and promoting the faster movement of transit traffic destined to or from landlocked member states.

Goals: Growth in the percentage of container shipments clearing at inland clearance depots or off-dock container freight stations, resulting in lower dwell times at seaport terminals and land borders and reduced transit times for containers traveling between seaports and the landlocked member states.

- Cooperation mechanisms

Strategies: BIMSTEC will encourage national trade facilitation committees in their efforts to plan and promote improvements in trade facilitation performance, together with the active participation of border agencies and the private sector. BIMSTEC will consider the formation of a customs coordination committee should there be demand from member states. BIMSTEC will also encourage regular exchanges between clearance authorities at borders and their partner land border posts.

Goal: National trade facilitation committees should include representatives from the private sector to address the broadening scope of trade facilitation with changes in trading methods and practices. BIMSTEC will establish a BIMSTEC customs coordination committee if requested by member states.

- Customs legislation

Strategy: BIMSTEC will encourage the modernization of customs legislation, either in the form of new or revised customs acts or by supporting rules and regulations to facilitate planned changes in customs practices and procedures designed to enhance performance.

Goal: Customs acts should be reviewed every 10 years and updated if they are not compliant with international agreements and best practices—unless this can be dealt with by regulations not requiring specific parliamentary endorsement.

- Mutual recognition agreements

Strategy: BIMSTEC will encourage member states to increase the number of mutual recognition agreements between them, particularly for regular import or export products requiring certification.

Goal: A 50% increase in mutual recognition agreements between member states by 2025 and 100% by 2030, using 2020 as the base year.

- Time-release studies

  Strategy: BIMSTEC will encourage member states to undertake time-release studies at their most important borders on a scheduled basis.

  Goal: Establishment of effective monitoring systems on improvements in clearance performance in member states based on the results of time-release studies.

Hard Infrastructure

- Land border infrastructure

  Strategy: BIMSTEC will encourage the prioritization of the construction of border infrastructure at main and secondary BIMSTEC land border crossings, based on their processing functionality, projected staffing levels, and future traffic demand.

  Goals: Modernization of all BIMSTEC primary land borders completed by 2025 and main supporting secondary borders by 2030.

- Inland clearance depots

  Strategy: BIMSTEC will encourage the further construction of inland clearance depots in member states by promoting their inclusion in national development plans and in discussions with relevant authorities and international development partners.

  Goal: An increase in the number of customs-approved inland clearance depots in all BIMSTEC countries during the period of the strategic framework.

- Land ports

  Strategy: BIMSTEC will encourage the construction of land ports designed to relieve congestion at border checkpoints and the provision of value-added services at these facilities if fees are levied.

  Goal: All primary BIMSTEC land borders should be supported by adjacent land ports or integrated checkpoints by 2030 to reduce queueing at the physical borders.

- Container freight stations

  Strategy: BIMSTEC will encourage the further opening of off-dock container freight stations to help reduce congestion within BIMSTEC seaport terminals.

  Goal: All large BIMSTEC seaports should be supported by licensed off-dock container freight stations by 2025 capable of handling both less-than-containerload and full containerload traffic.

- Testing stations and laboratories

  Strategy: BIMSTEC will encourage expanding the capabilities of testing regimes by increasing the numbers of laboratories in each BIMSTEC country and/or growing the capacities of existing facilities and improving their connectivity to borders to expedite clearances.

  Goals: The numbers and capacities of testing laboratories should be increased during the framework period, and online links established between the main laboratories and borders by 2025.

Trade Logistics

- Changes in trade logistics

  Strategy: BIMSTEC will encourage member states to respond positively to the use of advanced logistical systems designed to help reduce supply chain costs and transit times without compromising compliance levels.

  Goal: Developing and adapting trade facilitation practices to be able to handle advanced trading applications; this should be achieved through enhanced awareness by increasing stakeholder consultation.

- Linkages between national single window and port community systems

  Strategy: BIMSTEC will encourage member states to advance national single windows and port community systems covering the most important seaports and establish information and communication technology linkages between them.

  Goal: All large BIMSTEC ports should have port community systems or equivalents linked to national single windows by 2030 to enhance container tracking for stakeholders.

Cooperation and Capacity Building

- Regional cooperation

  Strategy: BIMSTEC will encourage active cooperation and support for other trade facilitation cooperation initiatives in the BIMSTEC region and may provide assistance where appropriate.

  Goal: Active cooperation between regional trade facilitation initiatives, thereby ensuring overall compatibility and eliminating possible duplication of programs.

- Mutual cooperation in capacity-building

  Strategy: BIMSTEC will encourage exchanges between trade facilitation authorities in the member states based on mutual cooperation to assist in capacity-building and skill transfers.

  Goal: Assistance in capacity-building through mutual cooperation between partner agencies, combined with additional support from the international agencies if deemed appropriate.

- Internal capacity-building

  Strategy: BIMSTEC will encourage the provision of internal capacity-building training to enhance the skills of personnel working on trade facilitation activities. Member states with advanced training capacities may provide training for personnel from other BIMSTEC countries.

  Goal: Increased numbers of internal technical training courses for trade facilitation personnel to raise the overall level of professionalism within their organizations and their ability to implement advanced processing techniques.

The implementation of the strategic framework should be guided by the following seven principles:

- Country ownership;
- Results orientation, combined with pragmatism;

- Flexibility and responsiveness to individual country needs;
- Reform and modernization;
- Active participation and involvement of the private sector;
- Partnerships with international development partners; and
- Mutual cooperation.

Implementing the strategic framework should be funded by the internal resources of BIMSTEC countries, supplemented by bilateral and multilateral resources as appropriate. Multilateral institutions actively engaged in trade facilitation initiatives in the region include the Asian Development Bank, the United Nations Economic and Social Commission for Asia and the Pacific, the United States Agency for International Development, the World Customs Organization, and the World Bank. All have indicated their commitment to providing financial and/or technical support for implementing elements of the strategic framework, subject to requests from the relevant national authorities. These organizations can also assist in getting the private sector more involved in trade facilitation initiatives. Increased engagement with international development partners can also enhance resource mobilization needed for implementing elements of the strategy and assist the BIMSTEC Secretariat in program coordination and monitoring if so requested.

There are two main options for monitoring progress in implementing the strategic framework and achieving its goals. The first is to establish a central monitoring body within BIMSTEC, possibly with technical assistance, that reports directly to the Secretariat. Annual data could be provided by each country through their national trade facilitation committees or their equivalent, collating information from national agencies. The second is for the BIMSTEC Trade Facilitation Working Group, currently engaged in advancing the BIMSTEC Free Trade Area agreement, to take on this added responsibility and report annually on progress achieved. It may also be possible to utilize the data compilation resources of other international or regional partner initiatives.

A midterm review of the strategic framework should be conducted in 2025 to take stock of the progress achieved and to adjust the timing of realizing the various component goals if needed. The volatility caused by the COVID-19 pandemic and other economic disruptions should have passed by then and normal trading activities resumed. The review could also be an opportunity to reappraise the component strategies and goals in light of subsequent events and market pressures encountered during the first half of the decade.

INTRODUCTION

The core functions of the Bay of Bengal Initiative for Multi-Sectoral Technical and Economic Cooperation (BIMSTEC) are to promote free trade and increase cross-border investments. Trade was one of the six sectors of BIMSTEC cooperation determined at its inception in 1997, done in recognition of the important role that trade plays in both national and regional economic growth. BIMSTEC has adopted a dual approach to tackling constraints to trade in the region. The BIMSTEC Free Trade Area Agreement is being specifically planned to help eliminate or minimize the tariff barriers that can constrain intraregional trade; while the parallel trade facilitation initiative is designed to address the nontariff barriers (NTBs) affecting both global and intraregional trade.

BIMSTEC is actively addressing tariff barriers through the forging of a framework agreement for a BIMSTEC free trade area. This was signed and came into force in 2004, and sets out the steps to address tariff and NTBs that will need to be undertaken to realize a BIMSTEC Free Trade Area Framework Agreement. The BIMSTEC trade negotiating committee , at the time of writing, has held 21 rounds of negotiations toward finalizing the agreements and protocols that will form the integral parts of the free trade area, including agreements on trade in goods and services, rules of origin, trade facilitation, and the protocol for amending the framework agreement.

Progressing free trade areas and free trade agreements, in general, have faced significant headwinds in recent years, sparked by trade disputes, such as those between the People's Republic of China (PRC) and the United States (US) and between the US and the European Union, the collapse of North American Free Trade Agreement, and Brexit. Given these tensions, the time lag between the signing of any BIMSTEC Free Trade Area Framework Agreement and its full implementation into a regional free trade area is not surprising. The agreement includes aspects of trade facilitation and recognizes the negative impact of residual NTBs on constraining the benefits inherent in BIMSTEC countries passing the agreement into law. In September 2019, BIMSTEC's Secretariat issued the latest revised draft text of the Agreement on Trade Facilitation for the BIMSTEC Free Trade Area Framework Agreement and two rounds of negotiation have taken place.

Trade facilitation initiatives in the region have so far generally focused on the gradual elimination of NTBs that adversely affect cross-border trading activity. They initially focused on land borders and improving the customs environment, although this approach has since broadened to include other border agencies. Constraints to improving the trade facilitation environment are those NTBs that directly result in higher costs incurred by the trading community. Estimates from empirical research on the impact of NTBs suggest they have become far more trade-restrictive than tariffs. This is in part because tariff barriers are fixed and known in advance and therefore are allowed for in traders' costings, whereas many NTB costs are variable and not necessarily included in advanced costings, thereby representing a significant trading risk.

Implementing trade facilitation reforms in the region should generate substantial benefits from the resulting increase in trade, thereby promoting economic growth. Coordination in improving trade facilitation across the BIMSTEC region should ensure that traders are not encumbered by the differing customs and other border agency formalities and requirements that are adversely affecting trading activity. It is hoped a BIMSTEC free trade area will eliminate many tariff barriers, but this needs to be supported by a better regional trade facilitation environment for minimizing or eliminating residual NTBs.

Trade facilitation planning within BIMSTEC has been addressed to date in the BIMSTEC Master Plan for Transport Connectivity and is also included in the BIMSTEC Free Trade Area Framework Agreement, with its supporting agreement on trade facilitation. The Secretariat recognizes the importance of trade facilitation within the BIMSTEC initiative—hence, the request to prepare a strategic framework identifying the requirements that will be needed to enhance trade facilitation activities in the region, supported by a regional mechanism to oversee the implementation of that framework.

The structure of this report highlights constraints to the region's trade facilitation environment and how these can best be tackled through the implementation of the strategic framework. The rest of this report aims to answer the following questions:

- Section 2: What is the current scope of trade facilitation and how has this changed in response to meeting the needs of the trading community?
- Section 3: What trade facilitation agreements in the BIMSTEC region should the strategic framework be compliant with and complement?
- Section 4: What are the main trade facilitation NTB's the strategic framework needs to encompass?
- Section 5: What is the structural basis and content of the strategic framework and how should it be implemented and monitored?
- Section 6: The BIMSTEC Trade Facilitation Strategic Framework 2030

The strategic framework in Section 6 has been prepared as a separate 26-page draft document so that, after its approval by the member states, it can be published if required as a discrete document, similar to the South Asia Subregional Economic Cooperation (SASEC) Trade Facilitation Strategic Framework 2014–2018. Appendix 1 assess the state of trade facilitation in each BIMSTEC country and Appendix II covers external perceptions of the region's trade facilitation performance based on international surveys.

Starting the work on the strategic framework during the COVID-19 pandemic was a challenge, given its impact on and the uncertainties it has created in trading activities in particular and the trade facilitation environment in general. Even so, this was also an opportunity to identify and promote the interventions necessary to address the "new normal" as it evolves. Countries have already had to introduce some modifications to their practices and procedures to continue the processing of trade during periods of severe restrictions, especially regarding medicines, health products, and food. The expected reduction in and disruption of overall trade movements in the short-term provides a window of opportunity to usher in the more advanced approaches to trade processing contained in international agreements, the implementation of which can be supported by capacity building. This is also an opportunity for additional investments in hard infrastructure, which would generate jobs in the important construction sector.

EXPANDING THE SCOPE OF TRADE FACILITATION

The common definition of trade facilitation is the streamlining of customs and border procedures to allow imports and exports to flow more rapidly across borders. This is broadly the approach that was used to promote the Revised Kyoto Convention on the Simplification and Harmonization of Customs Procedures by the World Customs Organization (WCO). Other international bodies, however, have much wider definitions:

- The United Nations Economic Commission for Europe defines trade facilitation as the "simplification, standardization and harmonization of procedures and associated information flows required to move goods from seller to buyer and to make payment."[1]
- The World Trade Organization (WTO) defines it as the "simplification, modernization and harmonization of export and import processes."[2]
- The WCO also defines it as the "avoidance of unnecessary trade restrictiveness by applying modern techniques and technologies, while improving the quality of controls in an internationally harmonized manner."[3]

The common themes in these definitions all relate to processing and procedures, predominantly of trade documentation. Trade facilitation in the BIMSTEC region under various international financial institutions (IFIs) initiatives and member state activities over the last 2 decades has concentrated on three key areas: investing in the modernization of border infrastructure, developing automated customs processing systems, and establishing customs cooperation mechanisms.

The most tangible activity has been the construction and rehabilitation of border facilities, land ports, and inland clearance/container depots (ICDs). These types of physical infrastructure are attractive to governments and IFIs since they demonstrate in a highly visible form the investment being committed to enhancing the trade facilitation environment. Such improvements are not specified in the definitions above, but all assume that better infrastructure results in better processing. Anecdotal evidence, however, suggests this is not necessarily the case, and that processing and procedures and infrastructure modernization are two separate subjects, despite their interrelationships.

---

[1] United Nations Centre for Trade Facilitation and Electronic Business. 2002. *Compendium of Trade Facilitation Recommendations.* Geneva/New York. https://unece.org/DAM/cefact/publica/ece-trd-279_compendium.pdf.

[2] World Trade Organization. Trade Facilitation Agreement – Introduction. https://www.wto.org/english/tratop_e/tradfa_e/tradfa_e.htm#I.

[3] World Customs Organization. *What is Securing and Facilitating Legitimate Global Trade.* http://www.wcoomd.org/en/topics/facilitation/overview/customs-procedures-and-facilitation.aspx.

Investing in automated customs processing systems has been significant, particularly in the last decade, although this is possibly less noticeable to the public. The impact of the advances in information technology within the trading community and border agencies has nevertheless been transformational in terms of clearance processing methodology and performance. Yet, these behind-the-scenes advances remain a work in progress as the application of automation in the trade facilitation environment expands.

Evidence suggests that the scope of ongoing trade facilitation programs in the region may be too narrow for future market needs, particularly as stakeholder demands have gradually changed in response to global and national trading environments. Trade facilitation is also evolving due to the successful implementation of measures relating to the areas mentioned earlier. New border facilities are being built, all customs authorities in BIMSTEC countries have automated processing applications, and customs cooperation mechanisms have been established in most member states. The need now is to determine where the focus of trade facilitation should be in the future.

Figure 1 identifies the changing emphasis within trade facilitation, illustrating the evolutionary processes for understanding that trade facilitation responds to actions already taken and ongoing demands by stakeholders. The "narrow sense" broadly represents the traditional approach to trade facilitation, concentrated on improving border processing and infrastructure.

Because of the successful implementation of trade facilitation in the narrow sense in recent years, IFIs have gradually broadened their assistance to include other border agencies, including those responsible for sanitary, phytosanitary, and trading standards, and have addressed the need for even more behind-the-border reforms, such as the demand for inland clearance depots, as well as concentrating on the further advancement of national single windows. This reflects the "broad sense" of the need to reduce trade costs, not only at the physical borders relating to customs activities but also trade costs in

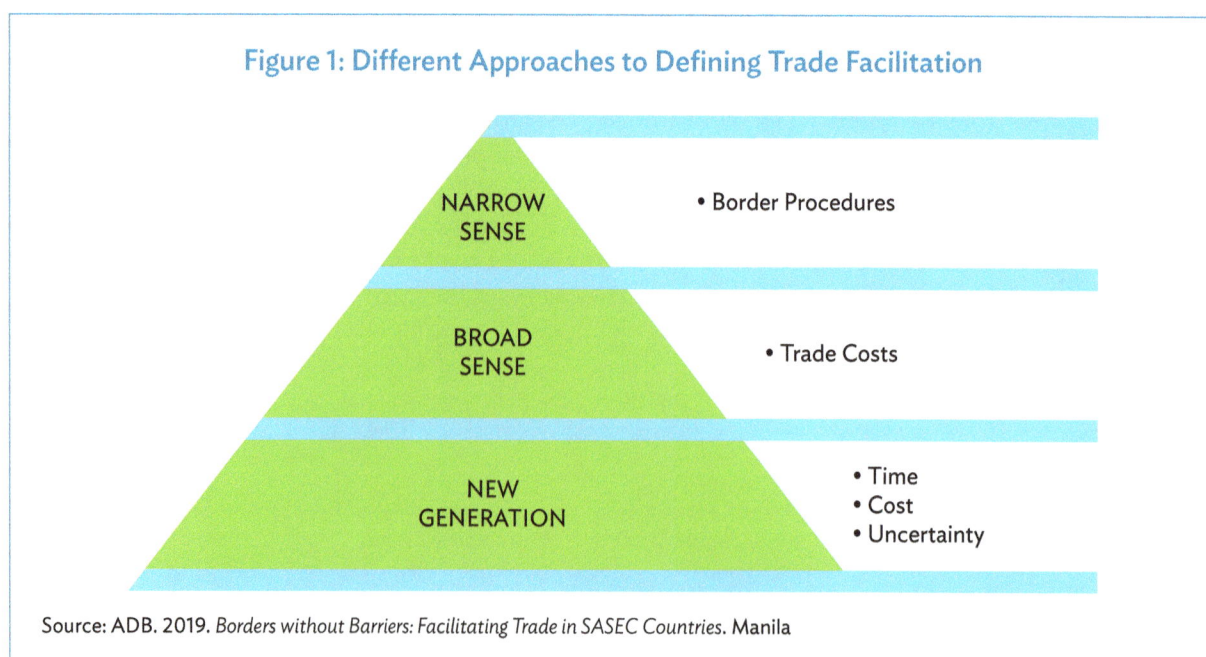

Figure 1: Different Approaches to Defining Trade Facilitation

NARROW SENSE — • Border Procedures

BROAD SENSE — • Trade Costs

NEW GENERATION — • Time • Cost • Uncertainty

Source: ADB. 2019. *Borders without Barriers: Facilitating Trade in SASEC Countries*. Manila

general. This suggests a gradual change of emphasis from trade facilitation predominantly being driven by the needs of border authorities to one being more oriented toward satisfying the demands of the wider trading community.

The Asia-Pacific Economic Cooperation has adopted an even broader approach to trade facilitation. This so-called "new generation" approach reinforces the change from the physical movement of goods through borders to the demands created by changes in the logistics environment, whereby the border transit merely represents a link within the overall international logistics chain. Modern trading activity involves concepts, such as just-in-time purchasing, which is designed to limit stock levels, and global value chains where various stages of production processing are located in different countries. These more advanced applications are dependent on three primary facets: time—transit times between supplier and purchaser; cost—overall charges incurred between supplier and purchaser; and reliability—dependability of the supply chain between supplier and end-user.

The relative efficiency of the trade facilitation environment in supplier and purchaser countries, as well as any transit counties, directly affects the potential to utilize these modern trading applications. Some BIMSTEC countries are already heavily dependent on just-in-time purchasing and global value chains in their international trade, especially India and Thailand, and to a lesser extent Bangladesh, Myanmar, and Sri Lanka. Even landlocked Bhutan and Nepal have these applications for a significant proportion of their localized cross-border trade. While all three facets are important, the most critical is probably reliability—that goods are delivered when and where they are supposed to arrive, thereby ensuring the continuity of GVCs production, minimizing stock levels in just-in-time purchasing, and ensuring customer satisfaction.

The scope of BIMSTEC trade facilitation needs to broaden beyond its traditional approach when compiling a strategic framework for the future. The various definitions of trade facilitation shown in Figure 1 have been adopted, and they provide the general parameters and set the boundaries proposed in the strategic framework. Core challenges that require addressing under the trade facilitation umbrella include compliance (i.e., promoting trade in a way that conforms to applicable rules and regulations), the needs of both border control agencies and the wider trading community (stakeholders) for hard and soft infrastructure development, enhanced processing with the greater application of automated technologies, additional behind-the-border facilities and procedures, and the ability to engage in more advanced trading and logistical concepts.

This widened scope encompassing the rationale of the broad and new generation definitions are compliant with, but not limited to, the specific trade facilitation strategies in the BIMSTEC Master Plan for Transport Connectivity, which is to:

- develop border infrastructure at the main BIMSTEC land border crossings,
- develop inland clearance depots at appropriate locations,
- review and rationalize documentation requirements for import and export clearance and promote mutual recognition agreements,
- upgrade automated systems within national customs administrations,
- establish national single windows, and
- adopt advanced logistical systems as an approach for reducing the high distribution costs and long transport times.

The strategic framework does not specifically cover constraints concerning through-transport agreements. This is because they are principally a transport barrier and would therefore be dealt with by BIMSTEC transport strategies. The absence of through-transport agreements can adversely affect the performance of trade facilitation, particularly in terms of additional costs and the time incurred in transshipping cargoes from one truck to another at borders. Accommodating these activities dictates the need for larger border and terminal facilities. Clearance procedures and processes relate to freight rather than the means of transport, and these are almost identical with or without through-transport arrangements. The main benefit of through-transport agreements is that they lower logistical costs and can enable goods to be cleared further inland from the border. Adopting and implementing through-transport arrangements will undoubtedly reduce transport costs to the trading community and are encouraged in BIMSTEC transport strategies. The strategic framework recognizes the need to have effective customs transit systems in place to accommodate through-transport as and where it is permitted in the future.

TRADE FACILITATION AGREEMENTS

In planning strategies to tackle nontariff barriers, it is important to be mindful of parallel actions designed to address tariff barriers. These barriers principally affect trade already taking place in the region. The unknown is the extent to which such tariff barriers are constraining trade that might otherwise have taken place or the impact on generating additional trade if such tariff barriers are to be eliminated—in other words, the potential to translate latent trade demand into actual demand. The following sections highlight some of the plans in the BIMSTEC region designed to address tariff barriers.

BIMSTEC Free Trade Area Framework Agreement

Member states have agreed to set up a BIMSTEC free trade area framework agreement to "stimulate trade and investment and to attract outsiders to trade with and invest in the region."[4] A trade negotiating committee was formed in September 2004, with Thailand as the permanent chair. The committee's negotiating areas cover trade in goods and services, investment, economic cooperation as well as trade facilitation, and technical assistance for the less developed member countries. It has been agreed that once the negotiations on trade in goods were completed, the committee would start talks on the trade in services and investment.

The BIMSTEC Free Trade Area Framework Agreement outlines the following areas to be addressed:

- Progressive and substantial elimination of tariff and nontariff barriers in all trade in goods;
- Progressive liberalization of trade in services with substantial sectoral coverage;
- Establishment of an open and competitive investment regime that facilitates and promotes investment within the BIMSTEC Free Trade Area;
- Establishment of trade and investment facilitating measures, including but not limited to the simplification of customs procedures and establishing mutual-recognition arrangements; and
- Establish mechanisms for implementation of the Framework Agreement.

The trade negotiating committee is currently in talks to conclude the following constituent agreements and a protocol that would form the integral parts of the BIMSTEC Free Trade Area Agreement:

- Agreement on trade in goods;
- Agreement on trade in services;
- Agreement on investment;

---

[4]   BIMSTEC. Free Trade Area Framework Agreement. https://bimstec.org/?page_id=205.

- Agreement on cooperation and mutual assistance in customs matters;
- Agreement on rules of origin and operational certification procedures;
- Agreement on trade facilitation; and
- Protocol to amend the framework agreement.

For the agreement on the trade in goods, two working groups were formed to work on the technical aspects: the Working Group on the Rules of Origin and the Working Group on the Dispute Settlement Mechanism. Both group meetings should be held back-to-back or parallel to trade negotiating committee meetings. It is understood that none of the agreements have yet been ratified and all are still being discussed. The latest version of the Agreement on Trade Facilitation for the BIMSTEC Free Trade Area was issued by the Secretariat on 30 September 2019. The specific objectives of this agreement are to:

- Achieve competitive and efficient movement of goods within the region to enhance BIMSTEC's trade and production networks to better participate in global value chains, and establish a highly integrated and cohesive economy;
- Address development gaps between and within the parties and the need to facilitate the increasing participation of all parties, especially the least developed country parties in implementing BIMSTEC trade facilitation programs;
- Enhance institutional coordination between the BIMSTEC sectoral bodies to implement trade facilitation measures under their oversight;
- Improve the monitoring mechanism for implementing trade facilitation measures; and
- Encourage the implementation of trade facilitation measures that have been accepted by international institutions, including the WCO and WTO, and in light of other relevant best practices.

Article 2 of the Framework Agreement notes the agreement only applies to cross-border trade facilitation between the parties. It is assumed that this includes all modes of transport and that a border could be a seaport or airport or a land border, and that the agreement also covers transit movements, even though these aspects are not specified. The Framework Agreement only addresses "customs procedures applied to goods traded among the parties and customs control on goods which enter or leave the customs territory of the parties."[5] This infers it is predominantly a customs-related agreement rather than one for comprehensive trade facilitation.

The institutional arrangements for the Framework Agreement, in article 16, stipulate that

- BIMSTEC shall establish a Trade Facilitation Committee comprising one nominee from each party, and it should meet at least once a year;
- The committee shall be supported by National Trade Facilitation Committees formed by the parties, and these will act in close collaboration with these committees; and
- The Trade Facilitation Committee shall review and facilitate the implementation and application of the Framework Agreement.

---

[5]   BIMSTEC. 2019. Second Meeting of the BIMSTEC Working Group on Trade Facilitation. Revised Draft of Text of the Agreement on Trade Facilitation for the BIMSTEC FTA. 29–30 September. https://bimstec.org/?event=second-meeting-of-the-bimstec-working-group-on-trade-facilitation.

The establishment of a BIMSTEC National Trade Facilitation Committee dedicated to monitoring the implementation of the above customs-related Framework Agreement differs from the role of any institutional arrangement to monitor the implementation of the BIMSTEC Trade Facilitation Strategic Framework 2030 that is expected to address a much broader interpretation of trade facilitation.

As noted earlier, the BIMSTEC Free Trade Area Framework Agreement has not been implemented, because many of its constituent agreements have yet to be approved. The trade facilitation agreement is still in its negotiating stages, whereas the Agreement on Cooperation and Mutual Assistance in Customs Matters for the BIMSTEC Free Trade Area is already in a final draft text format.[6] Because of this, the implementation of the Trade Facilitation Strategic Framework 2030 should not be conditional or dependent on the full implementation of the BIMSTEC Free Trade Area Agreement. Nevertheless, the Strategic Framework should be compatible with the sub-agreements within the Framework Agreement and acknowledge the benefits that a final BIMSTEC Free Trade Area Agreement should generate in the future.

South Asian Free Trade Area

The South Asian Free Trade Area (SAFTA) is the free trade arrangement of the South Asian Association for Regional Cooperation (SAARC). All South Asian members of BIMSTEC are members of SAARC and SAFTA. The agreement to set up SAFTA was signed in 2004 and came into effect in January 2006, to sustain mutual trade and economic cooperation among SAARC members through the exchange of concessions. The underlying principles behind the SAFTA agreement are:

- Overall reciprocity and mutuality of advantages to benefit equitably all members states, taking into account their level of economic and industrial development, the pattern of their external trade, and trade and tariff policies and systems;
- Step-by-step negotiation of tariff reforms, improving and extending them in successive stages through periodic reviews;
- Recognition of the special needs of least-developed member states and agreeing on preferential measures for them; and
- Inclusion of all products, manufactures, and commodities in raw, semi-processed, and processed forms.

Progress in implementing SAFTA has been partly impeded by a perceived lack of enthusiasm by some member states in this regional agreement, as opposed to existing bilateral arrangements. Another hurdle has been disputes between countries, particularly India and Pakistan, which are the grouping's largest trading members. It should be noted that, within the SAFTA agreement, changes require unanimous approval rather than a simple majority. SAFTA's intraregional trade share has remained largely stagnant, since the free trade area was set up, at 4.8% for intraregional imports and 7.2% for intraregional exports, with total intraregional trade at only about 5.9% of overall trade in 2019.

---

[6] BIMSTEC. 2018. *Agreement on Cooperation and Mutual Assistance in Customs Matters for the BIMSTEC Free Trade Area Agreement.* Dhaka.

The World Bank has identified some of the reasons limiting SAFTA's impact on increasing intraregional trade.[7] SAFTA has been undermined by the so-called sensitive list—a long list of products exempted from the tariff liberalization program. SAFTA countries have many products on their sensitive lists, ranging from 6% to 45% of their imports from other South Asian countries. Overall, only about 36% of trade in South Asia falls outside the preferential regime. Another reason is the proliferation of "para-tariffs," which are duties applied only on imports and not on domestic production. These tariffs increase overall trade protection, lack transparency, lead to dispersion of tariffs, and an overall anti-export bias of trade regimes where they prevail. They also fall outside the ambit of free-trade negotiations. These caveats all or in part adversely impact the scope and benefits of SAFTA.

Association of Southeast Asian Nations Free Trade Area

The ASEAN Free Trade Area (AFTA)[8] is a trade bloc agreement by ASEAN member countries to promote trade and manufacturing and facilitate economic integration. It is one of the world's largest free trade areas. ASEAN was formed in 1992, originally by six members, but now has 10 member countries, including BIMSTEC members Myanmar and Thailand. AFTA's primary goal is to increase ASEAN's competitiveness as a production base in world markets by eliminating tariffs and nontariff barriers within the bloc and attracting more foreign direct investments to ASEAN member countries.

The initial mechanism for achieving these twin goals was the Common Effective Preferential Tariff scheme that established a phased schedule in 1992 to increase ASEAN's competitive advantage as a production base geared for the world market. This was superseded by the ASEAN Trade in Goods Agreement in 2010. AFTA does not apply a common external tariff on imported goods, with each ASEAN member being able to impose tariffs on goods entering from outside ASEAN member countries based on their national schedules. Under AFTA, member states can apply tariff rates of 0%-5% on AFTA traffic and exclude certain tariff lines. AFTA's ultimate goal is to eliminate all tariffs except for certain tariff lines. The average ASEAN Trade in Goods Agreement tariff rate is believed to be 0.03%-0.04%.

AFTA has resulted in growth in intraregional trade well beyond 20% since 2010. Its progress in promoting this trade is through the implementation of the ASEAN Trade in Goods Agreement and other supportive agreements on investment, services, transport, and mutual recognition agreements. One of the reasons for AFTA's success has been the trade agreements signed by ASEAN with other countries, including India, Japan, the PRC, and the Republic of Korea, as ASEAN countries are highly dependent on global value chain trading activities. Most intra-ASEAN trade is supply chain-related trade in parts and components that mostly travel duty-free. The decision to multi-lateralize AFTA's tariff reductions has supported such trade because the final markets for finished goods are predominantly advanced economies outside Southeast Asia. Thus, AFTA's benefits have also been reflected in the external trade growth of ASEAN countries.

ASEAN has several free trade arrangements in addition to AFTA and these are combined into the Regional Comprehensive Economic Partnership (RCEP) covering ASEAN and all its six ASEAN Free

---

[7]   S. Kathuria. 2018. *A Glass Half Full: The Promise of Regional Trade in South Asia.* South Asia Development Forum. Washington, DC: World Bank.

[8]   ASEAN. 2002. Southeast Asia: A Free Trade Area. Jakarta. https://asean.org/wp-content/uploads/images/archive/pdf/AFTA.pdf.

Trade Agreement+1 Partners—Australia, India, Japan, the PRC, and the Republic of Korea. A free trade agreement between ASEAN and Hong Kong, China came into force in 2019. However, the RCEP signed in November 2020 did not include India at this stage.

Bilateral Agreements

In addition to regional free trade area agreements, BIMSTEC countries have bilateral free trade agreements with each other (Table 1). India and Thailand—the BIMSTEC countries with the highest volume of trade—are the most active in planning, negotiating, and implementing free trade agreements. BIMSTEC's landlocked countries, Bhutan and Nepal, only have agreements with their immediate neighbors. Myanmar appears to rely heavily on its membership of ASEAN for forging regional free trade agreements rather than negotiating separate bilateral agreements.

Table 1: Status of Free Trade Agreements among BIMSTEC Countries

FTA	Bangladesh	Bhutan	India	Myanmar	Nepal	Sri Lanka	Thailand
Number of FTAs	13	4	42	16	5	15	38
Bangladesh		P	P			P	P
Bhutan	P		S				
India	P	S			S	S	N
Myanmar							
Nepal			S				N
Sri Lanka	P		S				N
Thailand	P		N			N	

BIMSTEC = Bay of Bengal Initiative for Multi-Sectoral Technical and Economic Cooperation, FTA = free trade agreement, N = under negotiation, P = proposed or under consideration and study, S = signed and in effect.
Source: Asian Regional Integration Center. Free Trade Agreements (accessed 15 April 2021).

Impact of Free Trade Area Agreements in the BIMSTEC Region

When assessing the impact of free trade agreements in the BIMSTEC region, it is important to note that zero tariffs do not necessarily prevail on all trade between the members of regional free trade agreements. Most contain caveats designed to address sensitive goods and protect domestic industries, which can impact the effectiveness of these agreements. As noted earlier, the SAFTA agreement appears to have had a limited effect on South Asia's intraregional trade, which remains at about 5.5% of overall trade in 2017. ASEAN countries have seen a rise in their intraregional trade, in part because many member countries are active in global value chains; this is less the case in South Asia. Bilateral agreements appear to be more effective and potentially contain fewer caveats than regional agreements. For example, trade between India and Sri Lanka rose immediately after the implementation of a free trade agreement between the two nations.

There is a demand for forging both regional and bilateral free trade agreements, as evidenced by those being proposed and negotiated, but the pathway to implementation is complex and lengthy. The shift from globalism to protectionism has been a noticeable trend in recent years. While this has been most visible in US-PRC trade tensions, the renegotiation of the North American Free Trade Agreement and trade frictions between the US and the European Union are symptomatic of concerns over the "fairness" of international trade. This negative trend suggests that regional free trade agreements could become more difficult to agree on quickly, as countries seek to balance their national interests with those of the region. SAFTA's experience with sensitive lists and para-tariffs reflecting national interests can potentially compromise the effectiveness of regional free trade agreements in intraregional trade growth. In the short-term, bilateral agreements with fewer caveats might be more effective as "building blocks" for more effective regional agreements. However, a BIMSTEC Free Trade Area agreement, has the potential to generate more intraregional trade if tariffs, covering trade not already being included in bilateral agreements, can be reduced.

COVID-19 had an immediate impact on world trade, causing sharp reductions and disruptions of imports and exports globally and regionally. The medium- and longer-term effects are difficult to determine, especially with outbreaks of new strains. GVCs were in decline before the pandemic, which was another factor in multinational corporations reassessing their GVC models, particularly the problem in one supplier country adversely affecting the integrity of an entire supply chain. It is possible multinational corporations and large importers, in general, will increasingly look to more multi-sourcing to ensure product availability when trading systems are disrupted by seismic events in one country. The global financial crisis of 2008–2009 created a similar environment in which the virtues of GVCs were also under scrutiny. Regional free trade agreements in particular assist multi-country production and sourcing options, as shown within ASEAN. Thus, a BIMSTEC Free Trade Area agreement will be important not only for promoting intraregional trade but also for increasing the region's participation in GVCs.

The successful implementation of both regional and bilateral free trade agreements in reducing tariff barriers will further raise the importance of addressing NTBs. Recognition is growing that, as the tariff barriers come down through free trade agreements, the negative impact of NTBs become even more visible, and resolving them will be critical for realizing the benefits of implementing such agreements. Thus, the goal of increasing trade implicit in a BIMSTEC free trade area can only be achieved through enhanced trade facilitation in tackling NTBs in the region. It can be argued that tariff barriers at least represent a revenue benefit to governments, whereas NTBs generate economic losses to all parties.

TRADE FACILITATION ISSUES IN THE BIMSTEC REGION

This section examines the main trade facilitation-related issues in BIMSTEC countries that the strategic framework seeks to address. They are present in each country and are identified and discussed more fully in Appendixes I and II. There are inevitably differences in both the status of trade facilitation environments and the nature of the particular problems affecting individual countries. The strategic framework seeks to encompass common concerns wherever possible while acknowledging that their relevance will vary among countries given their differing trade facilitation situations.

Impact of COVID-19 on the Trade Environment

The pandemic and its after-effects continue to be the most immediate issue affecting trading activities in the region and impacting the BIMSTEC trade facilitation environment exposing any weaknesses. COVID-19 has hit all BIMSTEC countries, and each undertook mitigation steps to contain the spread of the disease, including lockdowns and border closures. The pandemic, in its early stages, tended to be mostly concentrated in developed countries, but then spread rapidly to developing countries across Asia, particularly impacting India and Bangladesh.

While the numbers of cases in the region were initially low in global terms, the World Health Organization warned against complacency, suggesting the pandemic may not have peaked in developing countries. This proved to be the case, especially in India and, to a lesser extent, Bangladesh, Myanmar, Nepal, and Thailand, where infection rates escalated rapidly. A significant second wave hit Europe and the US. The virus mutated into the more transmittable Delta and later Omicron variants, resulting in a significant increase in infections throughout the BIMSTEC region, in common with other world regions.[9] While vaccines have been gradually rolled out, it is clear some forms of remedial restrictions will likely remain well into 2022 and possibly beyond. It is unlikely that vaccine rollouts in the short-term will be sufficiently widespread to provide the necessary level of global herd immunity to reduce infection risks to a level sufficient to enable a full return to the pre-pandemic trading activities.

It is important to separate the impact of COVID-19 restrictions on trade and those on trade facilitation. A common factor between the two has been the closure of state and national borders that have highlighted any potential facilitation weaknesses. International trade was severely affected by these closures—not only by BIMSTEC countries but also by the border closures of their main trading partners. In some cases, movement restrictions applied only to passenger traffic, while freight was permitted to transit, albeit with additional checks. In general, freight movements through seaports were initially less affected, whereas freight movements by air were particularly severely affected early on by the lack

---

[9]   BIMSTEC had 38,831,618 cases and 535,856 deaths as of 5 October 2021, according to World Health Organization.

of passenger flights to convey most airfreight. International airfreight rates remain at near all-time highs and space availability continues to be limited. Significant disruptions of international supply chains have resulted in a shortage of containers and containership capacity, which, in turn, has hiked sea freight charges and delayed shipments. Although BIMSTEC countries have not generally imposed import and export restrictions on trade per se, certain restrictions were imposed on essential products.

Trade was expected to continue to be severely affected by the economic downturn, initially resulting from national restrictions to contain the spread of the pandemic. This extends far beyond the temporary border closures that have now been mainly lifted. All BIMSTEC countries except for Bhutan and Nepal are highly dependent on global, as opposed to regional, trading activity. The developed countries that account for most of BIMSTEC's primary export markets suffered temporary economic downturns, resulting in production closures and high unemployment levels. The emergency fiscal stimulus packages deployed to revive their economies largely focused on social aspects, including tackling rising unemployment and providing social safety nets for the poor through transfers. Low interest rates, backorders, and supply shortages created a temporary spike in demand for certain products, but the continued uncertainty is unlikely to allay a likely reduction in the overall demand for non-essential products, many of which are imported by developed countries either as finished goods or components. The result of this was expected to be a gradual reduction in overall spending on imports by global partners, particularly on "discretionary" products. Some BIMSTEC countries were looking at fiscal measures to support their export sectors, but this still requires demand from their import partners that may not necessarily be there.

The economic impact of national COVID-19 restrictions in BIMSTEC countries was also expected to lower their import demand, as each country struggled to tackle the economic and social impacts of these curbs, as well as growing fiscal deficits. Lower spending power resulting from the temporary decline in incomes and the ongoing constraints in the services sector inevitably impeded both supply and demand, including for imported products. Another issue that has still not yet been fully taken into account in many trade forecasts is the likelihood of a significant rise in bankruptcies from lost businesses during the pandemic. Many micro, small, and medium-sized enterprises, in particular, have been struggling to survive, as have service industries in their current form, for example in the tourism-related sector.

Trade in all BIMSTEC countries fell significantly in 2020. World trade was already falling in 2019 due to trade disputes among major trading countries. Data from the WTO showed global merchandise trade contracted by 5.3% in 2020, principally due to the COVID-19 pandemic; the WTO projected a rebound to 8.0% growth in 2021. Other forecasts suggest this growth would fall to 4.0% in 2022—still below the level of global merchandise trade before the pandemic. Since these various projections were made, the pandemic worsened in both developed and developing countries, suggesting appreciable downside risk associated with these forecasts.

Moving forward into 2021, trade demand started to re-emerge as developed countries came out of lockdown or restrictions were gradually being eased. The nature and speed of this recovery caused major supply problems. The first issue was producers and manufacturers had scaled back their operations due to the downturn in 2020 and were unable to suddenly increase their operations to meet the sudden surge in demand. This trend was exemplified by the semiconductor industry, which reduced the manufacture of microchips and when demand suddenly returned was unable to satisfy the market requirements, leading to other industries such as the auto and electronics industries having to reduce their production. The shortage of product against the surge in demand led to an ongoing worldwide shortage of certain products.

This sudden resurgence in demand created additional problems. Suppliers were working to supply back orders delayed by closures in 2020, while at the same time trying to satisfy new restocking orders in 2021. This state was then exacerbated by the publicity relating to delays in supply chains causing importers to order earlier than normal to ensure future stock availability. The shipping and port industry was unable to service this explosion in demand due to shortages of container vessels, containers, and road transport drivers to distribute containers to and from the ports. The result was severe port congestion in 2021 extending into 2022 and high freight rates that have significantly increased trade costs. By mid-2022, the situation had eased with sea freight rates gradually falling but some residual disruption in supply chains, especially with periodic lockdowns in the PRC continuing.

The longer the pandemic continues, the longer the recovery will be, especially if the Delta and Omicron variants continue to cause appreciable economic disruptions. The majority view was that a U-shaped recovery was much more likely in 2022, given the reduction in COVID-19 restrictions worldwide. Unfortunately, the fiscal measures taken to combat the COVID-19 downturn, especially low interest rates, have fueled inflation. Central banks are now raising interest rates to constrain demand and control inflation through the application of fiscal measures. At the same time, the sudden growth drove up energy costs that have been further exacerbated by the the Russian invasion of Ukraine and the resulting sanctions. These pressures suggest ongoing trade volatility with the specter of recession in some developed economies a realistic possibility. It is expected trade could take another 2 to 3 years to fully recover to 2019 levels.

The world is becoming increasingly oriented toward global consumption and international production networks using GVCs. Many developing countries in Asia are important suppliers of GVC products because of their low-cost operations. GVC trade represented more than 50% of global trade before the global financial crisis, but this share has fallen appreciably since then. The pandemic has resulted in a major disruption to supply chains, causing multinational companies in particular to re-evaluate their reliance on complex GVCs.

Many developing countries rely on GVCs for employment and growth and hence will be expected to be most impacted by changes in GVC patterns. Pressure is also increasing in developed countries to promote self-sufficiency or "manufacturing at home," rather than relying so heavily on cheaper production overseas. This is leading toward the concept of "gated" globalization, as opposed to unfettered market-led globalization, with more emphasis on multiple value chains or alternative supply chains to ensure greater reliability. The result of this re-evaluation will probably take some time to become fully apparent. GVCs involving low-value products are more likely to continue participating in these chains, but higher-value products may be more at risk. There is already anecdotal evidence that multinational corporations want to reduce their heavy dependence on their operations in the PRC and diversify sourcing options, especially as the PRC has indicated that it wants to reduce its dependence on exports in favor of stimulating domestic growth under its "common prosperity" strategy. These trends may present an opportunity to attract more GVC-type production to BIMSTEC countries.

In terms of trade facilitation, bottlenecks have been increasing at seaports, land ports, and ICDs. On the one hand, congestion has arisen due to traffic fluctuations caused by the pandemic while there have been trade facilitation problems in undertaking rapid border clearance processing due to a combination of personnel shortages within border agencies, difficulties for customs agents and brokers collating all the necessary documentation required to achieve a clearance, and the overall impact of national lockdowns and social distancing. Additional constraints have been experienced in obtaining import/export licenses, letters of credit, certificates of origin, and original bills of lading from the different issuing authorities.

Trade facilitation has not been at its best under these trying conditions, but with the expected temporary reductions in overall trade, many of these constraints will gradually be resolved. In some cases, the need for remedial action to tackle these problems has encouraged the application of the more advanced approaches that are included in the strategic framework. In India, for example, clearance processes have been simplified by relaxing the requirements for physical documentation, accepting e-gate passes, removing merchant overtime fees, reducing steps in the cargo clearance processing, not requiring original import general manifests, and waiving fees and penalties. India's Export Inspection Council has also advised that physical inspections should be avoided and consolidated shipments of essential cargoes are cleared on a trust basis. Customs are encouraging the advance filing of documents in their electronic data interchange platform before the goods arrive and have instituted online customs clearance for all priority and low-risk shipments on arrival. Customs also now accept e-signatures and e-mail authorized documents in cases where otherwise physical signatures would have been needed. The overall strategy of these measures was to promote physical distancing between border agency personnel and brokers, forwarders, and traders by increasing the use of information and communication technology (ICT).

Likewise, in Nepal to ensure the smooth functioning of customs offices by adopting the required safety protocols, Nepal's Department of Customs instituted a quick response team under the leadership of its deputy director-general of the Department of Customs with the mandate of resolving any deadlocks in the clearance of essential goods and to ensure the unhindered continuation of supply chains. It also put in place guidelines aimed at ensuring the expedited clearance of goods for the control and treatment of COVID-19. These guidelines among other things allowed for the deferred submission of papers required for customs clearance and also provisions for the establishment of a dedicated unit for the expedited clearance of essential goods. Other BIMSTEC counties have undertaken similar measures to address the operational pressures created by the pandemic.

Ironically, COVID-19 might offer increased opportunities to implement change during this initial period of lower demand for border clearances. This hiatus could encourage the trialing of new trade facilitation methodologies, updating ICT capabilities, making more personnel available for training, capacity-building, and improving cooperation between border agencies and the trading community.

Advancing Soft Infrastructure

The priority for improving BIMSTEC's trade facilitation environment under the "new generation" concept is to reduce the time and cost of border transactions, be they at land borders, seaports, airports, ICDs, container freight stations, or land ports. Enhancing the performance of border agencies will only be possible through procedural changes supported by investments in hard infrastructure. Ample evidence shows that investing in hard infrastructure at borders, seaports, and clearance facilities in isolation often fails to generate the anticipated facilitation benefits unless such investments are reinforced by parallel improvements in clearance performance by border agencies. The differences between countries with advanced border facilitation, such as Singapore, and BIMSTEC countries mainly relate to processing and procedures performance, rather than any lack of physical infrastructure.

Modern border processing is designed around the concept of gradually minimizing the interface between customs and other government agencies and the wider trading community, including agents, the objective being to promote "processing distancing" in a digital age. Clearances should eventually be predominantly online with limited face-to-face contact, which should only be necessary during the physical collection or cargo delivery for amber and red channeled shipments or in the case of disputes. All BIMSTEC countries have invested heavily in automation, particularly for customs. The principal objective of these IT investments has been to process more trade consignments without a corresponding need for additional staff. Declarations processed per year per officer is a common performance indicator, which has been rising in all BIMSTEC countries, principally due to increased automation.

The following subsections discuss the main constraints in the BIMSTEC region that were considered for inclusion in the strategic framework and which apply to all BIMSTEC countries to a greater or lesser extent.

Revised Kyoto Convention

The Revised Kyoto Convention has been adopted by all BIMSTEC countries. It was designed in 2006 as a blueprint for modern and efficient customs procedures. Its main principles include:

- Transparency and predictability of customs actions;
- Standardization and simplification of goods declaration and supporting documents;
- Simplified procedures for authorized persons;
- Maximum use of information technology;
- Minimum necessary customs control to ensure compliance with regulations;
- Use of risk management and audit-based controls;
- Coordinated interventions with other border agencies; and
- Partnership with the trade community.

The Revised Kyoto Convention is designed to promote trade facilitation and the implementation of effective customs-based controls through its legal provisions detailing the application of simple and efficient procedures. In principle, full compliance with the convention should address many of the soft infrastructure constraints discussed in the following subsections. The Revised Kyoto Convention consists of the main body text followed by a general annex, both of which are obligatory on accession to the convention. In addition, there are specific annexes covering non-mandatory practices and procedures, and compliance to elements of these specific annexes is dependent on individual country preferences. Three forms of implementation are specified: standard, transitional, and recommended. The standard clauses should be implemented within 3 years of accession to the Revised Kyoto Convention, whereas 5 years are allowed for transitional clauses. Nepal was the last BIMSTEC country to join the Revised Kyoto Convention in 2017. All other BIMSTEC countries should comply with the convention's standard and transitional requirements.

The main concerns over the Revised Kyoto Convention are that compliance can be open to differing interpretations and that many of the crucial procedural elements are contained in the non-mandatory-specific annexes. It could also be argued that the convention has been "overtaken" by the later WTO's Trade Facilitation Agreement (TFA) which is less customs-specific. Even so, implementing the Revised Kyoto Convention remains vital for enhancing customs practices and procedures.

In the context of the strategic framework, a caveat to the Revised Kyoto Convention is that, following initial accession, there is no ongoing reporting or published data on which of the important specific annexes have been implemented. Because of this, operationalizing various elements in the convention cannot be used as a potential monitoring mechanism. The WCO has useful support items, such as the convention checklist of general and specific annex provisions, but these are self-assessment checklists and hence not publicly available.

World Trade Organization Trade Facilitation Agreement

The WTO's TFA has become an international benchmark for modern trade facilitation practices. The Organisation for Economic Co-operation and Development (OECD) estimated that the agreement's full implementation would reduce trade costs in the BIMSTEC region by 10%-18%.[10] All BIMSTEC countries except Bhutan are signatories and are at varying stages of implementation (developed countries were expected to achieve 100% implementation on ratification). The implementation levels of BIMSTEC countries, estimated by the WTO in October 2021 are shown in Table 2.

Table 2. Implementation Levels of Trade Facilitation Agreement,
(as of October 2021)

Countries	Implementation Levels
Bangladesh	36.6%
India	78.2%
Myanmar	5.5%
Nepal	2.1%
Sri Lanka	31.5%
Thailand	97.1%

Source: World Trade Organization.

While Bhutan is neither a member of the WTO nor a TFA signatory, this should not prevent the country from adopting measures recommended in the agreement. Indeed, Bhutan has already adopted some measures in the agreement and, on a comparative basis, is thought to be at a similar level of implementation to Nepal.

A potential strategy could be phased compliance with the TFA as an important goal. The agreement's implementation for developing countries is categorized as A, B, and C, as explained below:

- Category A: provisions that signatories will implement by the time the agreement comes into force—within 1 year in the case of a least developed country;
- Category B: provisions that signatories will implement after a transitional period after the agreement comes into force; and
- Category C: provisions that signatories will implement on a date after a transitional period after the agreement comes into force and requires assistance and support for capacity building.

---

[10]   OECD. 2018. *Trade Policy Brief: Implementation of the WTO Trade facilitation Agreement: The Potential Impact on Trade Costs.* https://issuu.com/oecd.publishing/docs/implementation_of_the_wto_trade_fac.

Table 3 shows the notifications by governments indicating the status of implementation of each article of the TFA by category as recorded to the WTO. This mainly relates to notifications made to the WTO in 2018, in addition to updates from BIMSTEC countries, where available up to mid-2021. Further progress will likely have been achieved in many cases since their last reporting. Table 3 shows that BIMSTEC countries fall into three implementation categories. Thailand and India have high levels of compliance, followed by Bangladesh and Sri Lanka with mid-levels of implementation, and lastly, Myanmar, Nepal, and Bhutan with high levels of category C compliance signaling the need for external assistance, though they are making progress. For the strategic framework, it will be important to include elements of targeting and monitoring to be able to evaluate progress, based on the levels of implementation and achievement realized. The TFA could be a possible external monitoring methodology for the advancement of soft infrastructure.

Table 3: Compliance Status of BIMSTEC Countries Trade Facilitation Agreement

Country	Category A	Category B	Category C
Bangladesh	34.5	36.5	29.0
India	72.3	27.7	0.0
Myanmar	5.5	9.2	85.3
Nepal	2.1	44.1	53.8
Sri Lanka	29.0	1.7	69.3
Thailand	91.6	8.4	0.0

BIMSTEC = Bay of Bengal Initiative for Multi-Sectoral Technical and Economic Cooperation.
Note: Bhutan is not included since is it not a member of World Trade Organization and not a signatory to the Trade Facilitation Agreement.
Source: World Trade Organization. Trade Facilitation Agreement Database (accessed 15 October 2021).

The TFA's overall purpose is to expedite the movement, release, and clearance of goods. It contains implementation flexibility in the form of 35 non-mandatory technical measures. Some of these only require best efforts and allow each WTO developing member country to decide when it will instigate a measure and to determine the support needed for its implementation. Any target setting for implementing the TFA in the strategic framework needs to be realistic in terms of achievability, while also incorporating an element of pressure for reaching targets as early as possible. A target that is set too high or low will inevitably compromise its viability as a measure of success and targets in the strategic framework would have to be agreed upon by each BIMSTEC country before their inclusion. A big advantage of using the TFA for monitoring purposes is that it imposes minimal additional reporting, as all member states, except for Bhutan, have to submit notifications of their progress to the WTO. It is worth noting the ASEAN Trade Facilitation Framework that applies to Myanmar and Thailand is largely based on the implementation of the TFA.

The following could be potential strategic targets:

- India, Thailand — TFA; all Category B to A by the end of 2024
- Bangladesh, Sri Lanka — TFA; all Category C to A or B by the end of 2023 and all Category B to A by the end of 2026
- Myanmar, Nepal, Bhutan — TFA: 20% Category A, 40% Category B, and 40% Category C by the end of 202340% Category A and 40% Category B and only 20% Category C by the end of 2026

Its 35 measures are not of equal importance in achieving the overall goal of expediting the movement, release, and clearance of goods. Some measures have a greater impact on facilitating trade than others. The core articles are contained in section 1 (articles 1–12) of the agreement. The following are considered the most essential measures for expediting clearance times and reducing costs:

- Article 10.1   Formalities and documentation requirements;
- Article 10.2   Acceptance of copies;
- Article 10.7   Common border procedures and uniform documentation requirements;
- Article 10.4   Single window;
- Article 1.2   Information available through the internet;
- Article 7.4   Risk management;
- Article 7.5   Post clearance audit;
- Article 7.7   Trade facilitation for authorized operators;
- Article 7.1/2   Pre-arrival processing;
- Article 3   Advanced rulings;
- Article 11   Freedom of transit;
- Article 8   Border agency cooperation;
- Article 12   Customs cooperation;
- Article 23   Institutional arrangements; and
- Article 7.6   Average release times.

The soft infrastructure constraints present in the BIMSTEC region are discussed in groupings in the following subsections.

Rationalization of Clearance Documentation

Various SASEC and GMS studies in recent years examining the situation at BIMSTEC ports suggest dwell times for container traffic are often dictated by the time taken for importers or their customs agents to collect all the hard copy documentation to enable a declaration to be lodged with customs, rather than the actual physical customs processing times. Clearing and forwarding agents at both seaports and land borders often cite the collection, collation, and copying of these various support documents as their biggest problem.

The experience of other regions shows that reducing the number of hard copy documents needed to be presented for clearance reduces clearance times and transaction costs. ADB, WCO, and the World Bank, among other organizations, have sponsored national and subregional programs to address this issue in several BIMSTEC countries. Tables 4 and 5 show an outline analysis of the documentation requirements in each BIMSTEC country.

Table 4: Documents Required for Import Clearance in BIMSTEC Countries

Document	Bangladesh	Bhutan	India	Myanmar	Nepal	Sri Lanka	Thailand	Singapore
Declaration	X	X	X	X	X	X	X	X
Invoice	X	X[a]	X	X	X	X[a]	X	X
Packing list	X	X		X	X	X	X	X
Bill of lading	X	X	X	X	X	X	X	X
Letter of credit	X		X			X		
Certificate of origin	X	X				X	X	X
Insurance policy	X	X				X		
Import license		X		X		X[b]		
Sale contract				X				
VAT certificate	X							
Import permit				X				
Letter of authority					X			
Transit document					X			
Goods arrival notice								

BIMSTEC Bay of Bengal Initiative for Multi-Sectoral Technical and Economic Cooperation, VAT = value-added tax.
[a] Requires bank authorization/stamp
[b] Where appropriate
Source: National Customs websites.

Table 5: Documents Required for Export Clearance in BIMSTEC Countries

Document	Bangladesh	Bhutan	India	Myanmar	Nepal	Sri Lanka	Thailand	Singapore
Declaration	X	X	X	X	X	X	X	X
Invoice	X	X	X[a]		X	X	X	X
Packing list	X	X	X	X		X	X	X
Insurance certificate	X	X						
Letter of credit	X[a]	X		X				
Export form	X							
Taxpayer identity no.	X					X		
VAT form	X				X			
Export license		X		X		X[c]	X	
Purchase order		X						
Certificate of origin	X	X			X	X[c]		
Bill of lading			X	X				X
Let for export cert.			X					
Sales contract				X				
Shipping instructions			X	X				
Samples				X				
Foreign exchange documents					X			
Transit document					X			
Export permit						X[c]		X

BIMSTEC Bay of Bengal Initiative for Multi-Sectoral Technical and Economic Cooperation, VAT = value-added tax.
[a] Requires bank authorization/stamp
[b] Requires bank authorization/stamp where appropriate.
[c] for selected commodities for selected countries only.
Source: National customs websites.

Both tables suggest the documentary requirements for Thailand, the most advanced trade facilitation country in BIMSTEC, and Singapore, the Asian leader in this regard, are significantly less than those in the other BIMSTEC countries. The core documents required for imports or exports are a customs declaration, a pro-forma invoice, a packing list, a bill of lading, and a certificate of origin depending on the country of import/export. It is hoped that during the strategic framework period that the number of documents required for an import/export clearance will be gradually reduced to these core documents.

Surprisingly, more documentation is often required for exports than imports. Several BIMSTEC countries have export promotion schemes, requiring additional supporting documentation that is not included in Table 5. It may be that in some cases this situation could act as a disincentive to export.

Another constraint is the need to produce original documentation at the time of initial lodging. This requirement becomes particularly difficult if a document has to be authorized or stamped by an external party, such as a bank. Although customs declarations are lodged electronically by customs agents, brokers in most BIMSTEC countries also have to print out and sign an original when presenting in the "long room." The goal should be that all clearance documentation can be submitted in e-form with electronic signatures, as required. This would enable shipments to be processed solely based on documentation in the system, with originals only needing to be presented for cross-referencing when the goods are cleared for final dispatch.

Customs agents have long complained about the large number of copies of documents needed for clearance. In some BIMSTEC countries, customs declaration consists of up to seven copies, many of which are file copies for different clearance processes. Studies on the Bangladesh and Nepal borders draw attention to instances where over 30 originals and copies are required for a single clearance. Because all customs authorities have automated systems containing this information, the need for so many copies is questionable. As BIMSTEC countries increasingly move toward the e-filing of supporting documentation, the number of copies required should correspondingly be reduced.

Another problem is the lack of harmonization in the documentation required for a clearance, despite recommendations on this by the WCO and the Revised Kyoto Convention on the Simplification and Harmonization of Trade Procedures. Although automation has largely standardized the layouts of customs declaration forms, based on variants of the single administrative document developed in Europe, there has been little or no standardization of other documents, for example, those for sanitary, phytosanitary, veterinary, and trading standard requirements. BIMSTEC countries tend to have their own formats for these documents and the validity of non-nationally produced documentation is usually not acknowledged, thus requiring duplicate documents to be obtained from national agencies. The differing data requirements in these forms will inevitably make the forging of a regional single window more complex. There are international formats for quarantine, veterinary, and some trading standards documentation, but these are not widely used or accepted in the region.

Automation, National Single Window, and Trade Portals

Customs Information and Communication Technology Applications

All BIMSTEC customs organizations have computer systems for collecting and processing customs data:

- Bangladesh   Automated System for Customs Data (ASYCUDA) World;
- Bhutan   Bhutan Automated Customs System;

- India   Indian Customs Electronic Data Exchange System (ICES);
- Myanmar   Myanmar Automated Cargo Clearance System;
- Nepal   Automated System for Customs Data (ASYCUDA) World;
- Sri Lanka   Automated System for Customs Data (ASYCUDA) World and
- Thailand   E-Customs.

Data required for clearances are submitted by authorized customs brokers, forwarding agents, or approved service centers that prepare entries for smaller brokers who lack online access. All these customs systems record the data needed for a standard declaration (sometimes referred to as a bill of entry or a bill of export), but significant differences exist in the processing capabilities of these systems. In some cases, this is due to the limited application of additional modules within the system or to problems relating to day-to-day processing capabilities.

In some BIMSTEC countries, these systems are sometimes used to merely record transactions rather than assist in the automated processing of clearances (i.e., the system is used as a data repository rather than an operating tool). As noted earlier, declarations are made online, but entries are often validated only when they are lodged by the signing of printouts and the submission of hard copies of supporting documents. Frequently the clearance process is done using the traditional manual system of officer authorization signatures being required during the various stages of the clearance process until the goods are finally released.

A challenge in some instances is that certain personnel have not fully bought into the system and feel more comfortable using traditional manual control methodologies. For them, automation has sometimes been seen as a threat, rather than making their tasks easier. Stakeholders complain about manual and automated systems operating in parallel, resulting in increased workloads. This is a particular problem at the smaller land borders, rather than at larger ports or border posts. Most of these systems have processing modules, but often they are not fully applied, and the perception is that overall clearance times have not decreased appreciably as expected with automation. These systems are designed to not only improve performance but also to make tasks easier for officers by providing them with the right processing tools. Unfortunately, these applications are not always being used to their optimum capabilities.

Automation by Other Border Agencies

While customs authorities have invested heavily in automated processing systems, this is not necessarily the case with other border agencies. The immigration authorities, border guards, and police all have separate ICT systems, which are calibrated to process passenger, rather than freight, traffic. Other important border agencies include quarantine, veterinary, and trading standards. In some BIMSTEC countries, not enough investment in IT has been made in these other agencies, which come under the jurisdiction of various ministries. Several reasons seem to explain this situation, including that their border activities do not generate sufficient income to justify the investment, the absence of off-the-shelf international systems, and their limited ICT use in general. Clearance problems by these agencies tend to be the primary cause of the longest delays at borders. The implementation of national single windows (NSW) is bringing the need for investing in ICT systems at these agencies to the fore.

National Single Windows

The application of NSWs is the next big phase for automating trade facilitation. An electronic single window is a facility that allows all parties involved in trade clearances to lodge standardized information and documents at a single electronic data entry point to fulfill all import, export, and transit-related regulatory requirements. If information is in electronic format, individual data elements should only need to be submitted once. In essence, all documentation and information required by border agencies become available online within a single database, so that each party can clear shipments electronically and the customs administration that authorizes the final release can verify that all other agencies have approved the clearance. The benefits of NSWs are substantial and most BIMSTEC countries are either using them or are committed to advancing these systems. The NSW concept is shown in Figure 2 below.

The slow implementation of NSWs in the region testifies to the challenges—and there are three main ones—in setting up these complex applications. Firstly, it is essential to have a stable customs ICT system to act as the core of any NSW system. Secondly, as already noted, many other border agencies have significantly lower use of ICT systems than customs, and most do not generate computer certifications online. This makes it particularly difficult for these agencies to link up with the NSW. And thirdly, the biggest problem going by international experience has been institutional rather than technical. Setting up NSW planning committees and agreeing on the scope of participation has not been easy and this has delayed implementation. Some external parties perceive NSWs as a potential threat to their independence and their perceived role as "national protectors" of the borders.

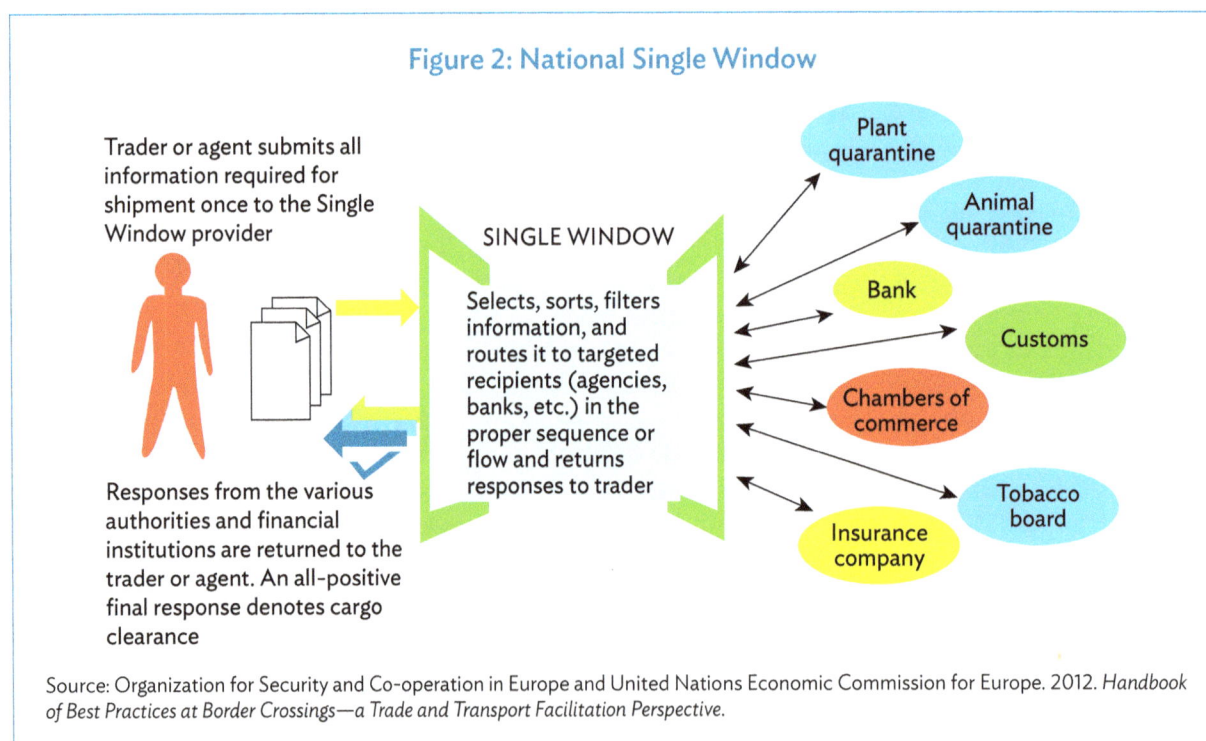

Figure 2: National Single Window

Trader or agent submits all information required for shipment once to the Single Window provider

SINGLE WINDOW

Selects, sorts, filters information, and routes it to targeted recipients (agencies, banks, etc.) in the proper sequence or flow and returns responses to trader

Responses from the various authorities and financial institutions are returned to the trader or agent. An all-positive final response denotes cargo clearance

Plant quarantine
Animal quarantine
Bank
Customs
Chambers of commerce
Tobacco board
Insurance company

Source: Organization for Security and Co-operation in Europe and United Nations Economic Commission for Europe. 2012. *Handbook of Best Practices at Border Crossings—a Trade and Transport Facilitation Perspective.*

These difficulties notwithstanding, establishing NSWs is an important BIMSTEC trade facilitation goal, and progress is being gradually achieved. Thailand has an NSW and is pursuing its National Single Window Vision 2021 with linkages to an ASEAN single window. Figure 3 shows Thailand's NSW and the complexity of building this system, which handled 148 million messages in 2019 and is linked to 39 parties.

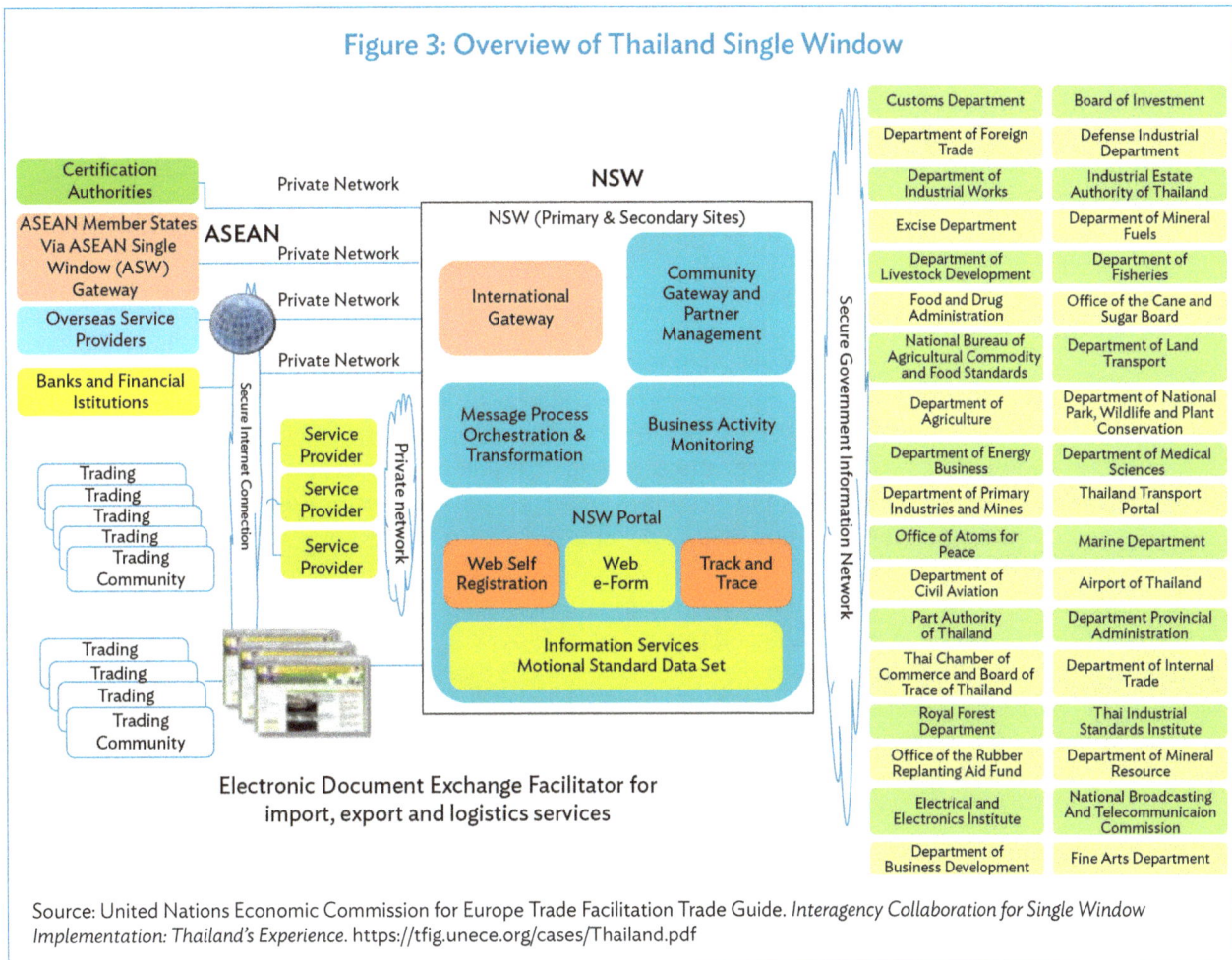

Figure 3: Overview of Thailand Single Window

Source: United Nations Economic Commission for Europe Trade Facilitation Trade Guide. *Interagency Collaboration for Single Window Implementation: Thailand's Experience.* https://tfig.unece.org/cases/Thailand.pdf

The coverage of India's single window interface for trade has expanded rapidly and now covers 62 agencies. The involvement of so many agencies highlights the complexity of their trade facilitation environment and the need for extensive coverage to develop a single window to include all interested parties, such as export promotion and industrial organizations. Using the integrated declaration, India's customs ICT system automatically identifies import and export goods requiring clearance by the participating government agencies for processing. The single window interface has so far eliminated the need for nine different documents.

Bangladesh was planning to launch its NSW by 2021 with the assistance of World Bank funding. It will be linked to 39 ministries, government agencies, and other organizations. Its full implementation has recently been revised to 2024. Nepal formally launched its NSW in January 2021. Its system is linked to 27 agencies and stakeholders and is expected to be linked to its target of 40 agencies. Sri Lanka is preparing a NSW blueprint, with technical assistance from the World Bank. It currently has a modified form of single window covering some agencies, but it does not link customs directly with all the other border agencies. Bhutan is the only BIMSTEC country that has not yet started on an NSW, although one is planned.

NSWs are still a work in progress in many BIMSTEC countries. The difficulties in setting them up should not be underestimated, particularly in getting the diverse border agencies on board to participate in the joint venture. But the more agencies that are involved, the greater the benefits to the trading community. Despite the challenges, developing NSWs should be endorsed as part of the strategic framework. The implementation of an NSW can be a gradual process that links customs with a few of the other key border agencies and then expands as other agencies acquire the necessary technology to be able to link into the system. In other words, start small and expand, rather than delay the start by applying a 'big bang' approach.

Trade Information Portal

A common problem in many BIMSTEC countries is identifying exactly what are the documentary and regulatory requirements in trading to ensure compliance. Automated clearance systems and trade facilitation, in general, is all about compliance—that is, traders or their representatives comply with the requirements to get their imports and exports cleared. A common problem has been that the traders do not know exactly what these requirements are, how to interpret the regulations, and where this information can be readily accessed. This situation is especially pertinent to South Asia, which has large numbers of small traders, one-time importers, and exporters with limited trading expertise.

Most BIMSTEC countries now have trade information portals. In Bangladesh, it is managed by the Ministry of Commerce. Bhutan's is managed by the Ministry of Economic Affairs, but it only covers exports and is more oriented toward export promotion—and is therefore not a trade information portal in the conventional sense, although it is being further developed. India has a comprehensive trade information portal managed by the Department of Commerce that is similarly oriented toward exports but also includes some information on imports. Myanmar's portal is managed by the Ministry of Commerce and covers all trading activity. Nepal's was launched in September 2019 and principally facilitates exports, although it also includes some information on import requirements. Sri Lanka launched its trade information portal in July 2018 with technical assistance from the World Bank and it is managed by the Department of Commerce. Thailand's National Trade Repository website acts as a trade information portal and is managed by the Ministry of Commerce's Department of Trade Negotiations. All BIMSTEC countries are compliant with trade information portal requirements, but in some cases, further expansion may be necessary, especially in covering import information.

E-Trading

Significant ICT advancements have taken place within customs. The primary role of customs, as set out in the Revised Kyoto Convention, is to facilitate compliant trading activity. This is also true to a large extent of other border agencies, although most still retain the control function as their primary remit. Both customs and these other agencies need to respond to changes in the way international trade is conducted in the future. ICT will play an ever-increasing role in trade, as with business in general. This will involve refinements in international logistics (the way trade moves); the use of different trading terms, such as cost, insurance, and freight, free delivered, ex-works, and free-on-board; and the growth of e-commerce and e-trade. It will be important that the ICT systems used by border agencies adapt to these changes and be ready to respond to tomorrow's trade environment, rather than solely resolving today's constraints. Cooperation mechanisms with the trade community, which are discussed later, should help identify these changes at an early stage and enable technical advancements by border agencies to respond to the external trading market's needs.

Risk Management and Authorized Economic Operators

Risk Management

An important recommendation in the Revised Kyoto Convention is the application of risk-based controls via the WCO's SAFE Framework. This is endorsed in Article 7.4 of the TFA. This procedure recognizes that as trade expands it will not be physically possible to examine every shipment without causing severe congestion and delays at the seaports and borders. It also recognizes that most shipments are likely to be compliant, especially those of regular traders. The risk management system is designed to facilitate the movement of cargoes of compliant traders by identifying which shipments present a risk and need to be examined and those that can be cleared solely based on documentary controls. In effect, this procedure provides a channeling methodology for identifying which shipments need to be inspected or examined. Standard channeling approaches are:

- Green: Shipment cleared without the need for physical inspection;
- Amber: Examination of documentation required before deciding on green or red channel; and
- Red: Shipment requires further documentary and physical inspection.

Most automated customs control systems have risk assessment applications or selectivity criteria in their software. Although the concept of risk assessment is generally accepted by all the BIMSTEC customs, high levels of examination prevail in many countries. The inspection and examination processes are the cause of the longest dwell time within a clearance. This is not only due to the high levels of examination but also because there is often a shortage of examination officers relative to the inspection workload. It is accepted the large numbers of small traders, especially in South Asia, can potentially compromise the benefits of risk management and result in more amber or red channeling. In general, customs channeling is practiced at BIMSTEC seaports, but it is often less prevalent at land borders, especially those with lower throughputs.

Authorized Economic Operators

An extension of the risk management concept is that of "trusted traders" or authorized economic operators (AEO). The logic behind this approach is that large regular traders, such as multinational corporations and major corporations, represent a low non-compliance risk and this should be reflected in higher service levels and enhanced facilitation. These organizations can apply to become trusted traders based on their records of compliance. If approved, they are generally exempt from regular examinations (i.e., categorized as green channel) other than from random checks to reconfirm compliance.

According to the WCO, AEO programs are only fully operational in India and Thailand. Bangladesh customs indicate they have an AEO program in place with supporting legislation, although only three pharmaceutical companies have yet approved AEO status. Bhutan has no AEO program but is piloting a compliant trader program with three importers. Myanmar tried to implement an AEO pilot program during the pandemic and is proceeding with implementation in 2022, with mutual recognition with partner countries in 2025. Nepal has legal provisions for authorized operator programs in a new draft customs act that has been submitted to the Parliament. The AEO program of Sri Lanka customs is governed by an AEO committee which has been appointed by the director-general of customs under a departmental order.

The principle of AEOs is accepted in all BIMSTEC countries. ADB, UNESCAP, the WCO, and World Bank have all provided training programs on AEOs and the SAFE Framework. The strategic framework should encourage the more widespread application of this processing approach, despite it not being specifically mentioned in the BIMSTEC Master Plan for Transport Connectivity.

Post-Clearance Auditing

An important support mechanism for risk management and AEOs is post-clearance auditing. Here, imported goods are green channeled, enabling rapid clearance from seaports or borders on the condition that customs can later examine the documentation and/or the shipment post-clearance at the importer's premises if deemed necessary. In Thailand, customs officers may enter a firm's premises for a post-clearance audit up to 5 years from the date of import or export. In most cases, this would only be a documentary audit, as the goods would probably no longer be available for physical examination.

In 2011, India limited the concept of a post-clearance audit to certain categories of importers and exporters. In 2018, the government strengthened the legal ambit of post-clearance audits through statutory amendments and notifications. This led to the formation of the Audit Commission, which operates at the largest seaports, and the issuing of comprehensive guidelines on post-clearance auditing. It is believed that post-auditing has not yet been widely extended to land border traffic.

In Bangladesh, the WCO through the SASEC program provided diagnostic training in 2019 to enable the implementation of post-clearance auditing in the following year. In Sri Lanka, customs have established a Compliance and Facilitation Directorate with a post-clearance audit branch in line with WCO and TFA requirements and ADB has provided technical support. A standard operating procedure has been drafted and is to be published. In Myanmar, post-clearance auditing was implemented in 2017 based on the Sea Customs Act. Here, auditors can enter business premises and examine trading documents on any shipment within the last 7 years. The audit is carried out both on-site and through desk audits in accordance with WCO post-clearance audit principles. Nepal's Department of Customs has its Post Clearance Audit Office in operation. In Bhutan, the customs rules and regulations include provisions for port-clearance auditing.

All BIMSTEC countries have either post-clearance auditing in operation or are continuing to train officers in this procedure. The WCO recognizes this is a specialist area requiring skills differing from those needed for traditional customs activities. This may be a limiting factor for the increased use of post-clearance auditing, especially in smaller countries where staffing is an issue or where there are institutional job rotation policies. Anecdotal evidence suggests many traders prefer getting full clearance at borders, rather than risk disputed extra duty on previously cleared goods. This is because customs officers may amend the value declared and initially accepted if these values are later found to be insufficient following an audit.

Pre-Arrival Processing and Advanced Rulings

Pre-Arrival Processing

The traditional approach to clearance still prevailing in BIMSTEC countries is that when a shipment arrives at a border, be it by land, sea, or air, the customs broker or forwarder enters an import or export entry declaration into the customs IT system. The broker then goes to the customs house and submits a signed hard copy of the documentation and supporting paperwork. An examination officer is then assigned if necessary. When the shipment is approved, the broker returns to the customs house and hands in the inspection approval, pays the duty, gets a release note, and arranges transport to remove the shipment. This process can take hours or even days, particularly if there is a shortage of examination officers relative to the number of shipments requiring inspection.

Various advanced techniques designed to expedite this cumbersome process exist. These include simple applications, such as pre-arrival processing, whereby an importer or exporter submits the declaration and documentation in advance of the physical arrival of the shipment. Thus, the process starts earlier and consequently facilitates a faster clearance when the goods physically arrive. Combined with risk management and AEO programs, pre-arrival processing can enable direct delivery or at least minimize clearance dwell times.

Pre-arrival processing at land borders and land ports is more difficult due to the short time between the dispatch of goods and their arrival at borders for processing. The exception is transit cargoes—for example, shipments through Indian ports to landlocked Bhutan and Nepal. Data can be entered with Bhutan and Nepal customs on arrival at Kolkata or Haldia, thus expediting the processing at the exit Indian land border, as well as at the borders of both landlocked countries. For maritime trade, the lead time from loading onto the vessel to its arrival at a seaport in a BIMSTEC country varies greatly, from 2–3 days to 2–3 months depending on the seaport of origin and whether transshipment is required. In these cases, the importer generally has much of the required information well in advance of a ship's arrival and can make a declaration, including providing most of the supporting paperwork.

Thailand introduced pre-arrival processing in 2019, as did Bangladesh, with shippers expecting to save nearly a week in receiving consignments. The import general manifest is submitted to customs as soon as a vessel leaves the overseas seaport. Sri Lanka Customs sent a draft of necessary amendments relating to pre-arrival processing to the Ministry of Finance in 2019 but approval is yet to be received. The other BIMSTEC countries have no pre-arrival processing system, although some allow declaration data to be entered into their customs computer systems. Even so, no actual processing is done before the goods physically arrive and confirmed declarations are lodged.

Advanced Rulings

Advance rulings are another common application, whereby a shipper or importer submits details of its shipments being traded and obtains a ruling that classifies the harmonized system coding of the product, its origin, and/or its value. This helps eliminate later disputes at borders during assessment and examination. Disputes over value and product coding are relatively common throughout the region. An advanced ruling facilitates the clearance of goods; this is because one of the primary reasons for examinations is assessing whether the product coding or value is correct. Advanced rulings also enable importers to validate their self-assessments and duty liabilities when entering declarations. Advanced rulings tend to have expiry periods, varying from 3 months to a year.

Bangladesh introduced advanced customs rulings in 2016, but these were restricted to product coding classifications. To date, there have only been 17 rulings. Bhutan introduced advanced rulings following training by the WCO in 2018, but, again, this is only for harmonized system coding. In India, the 2018 budget proposed amendments to the Customs Act of 1962 to not only enhance the scope of the advanced ruling system but also to revamp procedures. Importers and exporters can seek advance rulings on matters beyond the classification of goods, such as the applicability of notifications on duties to be paid, and valuation.

Myanmar has had advanced rulings on classification and valuations since 2014. Nepal's advanced rulings have been approved with legal provisions that came into effect in February 2020. Sri Lanka has had advanced rulings on product classification for some years. In March 2020, the WCO provided training on the new advanced origin rulings that were expected to be introduced in 2021. The Thai Customs has advanced ruling procedures. A December 2019 WCO workshop focused on uniformity in the interpretation and application of the harmonized system nomenclature and introduced amendments to the harmonized system coding that will come into force in 2022.

Transit Systems

The modern trend in the clearance of imports is to transfer the main cargo clearance procedures from the points of entry, either a land border or seaport, to inland locations, such as ICDs or bonded warehouses closer to the importer or end-user. This approach facilitates trade because the clearance process takes place in the centers of inland demand, making it easier for consignees or their agents to lodge supporting documentation. More importantly, congestion risks at border points of entry are reduced, because cargoes can move quicker through borders or seaports to inland facilities. Inland clearance is becoming increasingly important for dealing with congestion at container terminals in the BIMSTEC seaports. This approach requires the development of transit mechanisms for the inland movement of uncleared cargoes, be it in a container or a sealable vehicle.

The standard transit system used in developed countries is that movements travel inland under bond. Under this system, importers or their agents lodge a bond or deposit payment with customs, and the goods can then move from a border or seaport to an approved inland location for final clearance. The duty liability is covered by the bond, whereby if the goods are not delivered to the approved location and come into free circulation, customs can recover the duty that would have been payable from the bond payment. Importers or their agents can move several consignments at a time, with a total liability of up to the value of the bond lodged. The bond is released when a consignment reaches the inland location and is presented to customs, thus enabling the importer or agent to move additional shipments. All transit shipments are customs-sealed at the point of entry and the seal is broken by customs on arrival at the approved inland destination.

This well-established system is dependent on three elements: trust, finance, and security. Firstly, that the importers or their agents are reputable and the cargo is consequently considered less likely to disappear. Secondly that the importers or their agents have sufficient funds to lodge bond payments, either as a cash deposit or bank guarantee. Thirdly that the movement between a border or seaport and an inland location is carried out in a sealed unit and the cargo is secure so that it cannot be stolen during the inland transit. In developing countries, particularly with large numbers of small importers and agents, it is acknowledged that the proportion of imports that can meet these parameters may be more limited.

A similar regime can be applied to international transits, whereby cargo is landed in one country but is destined for another, such as cargoes for landlocked Bhutan and Nepal passing through the ports of Kolkata, Haldia, and Visakhapatnam. Another future route could be from eastern India to western India and vice versa through Bangladesh. It is understood some transit arrangements between Chattogram port and India's north eastern states have recently been arranged. This could also apply to some container shipments from Laem Chabang or Bangkok to the Myawaddy border in Myanmar.

Inland transit can be promoted in several ways. Many inland container depots (ICDs) are rail connected, thus facilitating the rapid movement of containerized traffic inland from seaports. In this case, the custodian of the cargo in transit is usually the state railway authority, which acts as the bondholder. The railways can offer a form of sovereign guarantee, thus meeting the trust and financial criteria—and rail shipments are anyway considered more secure than road transport. This transit mechanism is applied to all rail shipments in containers from Indian ports to approved inland ICDs and in Bangladesh from Chattogram port to the Dhaka ICD. It also applies to similar rail shipments from Kolkata/Haldia to the Nepalese border's Sirsaya ICD and rail container traffic between Laem Chabang Port and the Lat Krabang ICD in Bangkok.

The greatest transit risks relate to the movement of import cargoes by road, particularly from land borders. For containerized cargoes, these units can be sealed although there are residual issues such as whether or not the road networks can accommodate the weight or axle load of vehicles and their cargoes, such as in Bhutan and parts of Bangladesh. However, the key problem relates to the security of the road transport movement. Many inland transits in the BIMSTEC region travel along roads that have potential security concerns, particularly when overnight stops are needed. In these situations, the bond liability is significantly greater. For land borders, the "transit" from the border is more often in vehicles that cannot easily be sealed, and the cargo is generally in loose format and therefore more vulnerable to pilferage.

An electronic cargo tracking system, trials supported by ADB, has been promoted for containerized traffic to BIMSTEC's landlocked countries, Bhutan and Nepal, through Kolkata and Haldia ports by road. Under this approach, the containers are sealed with both a standard customs seal and an electronic seal. Shipment can be monitored by India's customs throughout its journey using data from the electronic seal, thus providing sufficient security to obviate the need for bonding. This system is also being trialed in Bangladesh, although its potential is more limited because it requires a sealed unit, such as a container, and this is not a route where containers are commonly used. The road transit of containers from seaports under bond is allowed in Thailand and short-distance transits by road in some parts of India. Imports into Bangladesh, Bhutan, Myanmar, Nepal, and Sri Lanka are almost exclusively cleared at borders, except for rail shipments to the Dhaka and Sirsaya ICDs and transfers to Yangon's off-dock ICDs and container freight stations (CFSs). Nepal has amended its Customs Act to allow inland transit to the new ICD at Chobhar in Kathmandu.

Despite these constraints in parts of the BIMSTEC region, pressure is increasing for more inland clearances to reduce the risk of congestion at terminals, land borders, and seaports. This can only be achieved if the three criteria cited earlier are met. This will require establishing automated transit systems particularly to address security. India's electronic tracking system is an example of this application and most customs ICT systems have transit modules, although they are not necessarily in operation. This may also require providing customs checkpoints or approved secure Transport International Routier-type parking depots along major routes.

Institutional Cooperation

Border Cooperation

Cooperation between border agencies is vital to achieving optimal clearance performance. This cooperation tends to be higher at small land borders because of the fewer numbers of personnel present, but becomes increasingly difficult at the larger borders, particularly where the individual authorities have separate facilities and buildings. Brokers have long complained about having to "run around town" to various authorities involved in clearances. Implementing NSW should help resolve some of these challenges. Because a clearance is a joint undertaking with each player taking a part, this must be a coordinated and cooperative team process. The TFA encourages these parties to meet regularly to ensure compatibility of clearance processing activities and address internal constraints as they arise.

The agreement also encourages officials on either side of land borders to meet regularly. Discussion areas include agreeing on the alignment of procedures and formalities, working days and hours, development and sharing of common facilities, the possibility of joint controls, and establishing one-stop border post controls. Aligning hours is particularly important at the India-Bangladesh, India-Nepal, India-Bhutan, and Thailand-Myanmar borders, where appreciable traffic imbalances exist. This can result in uneven demand for processing as traders clear on the Indian or Thai side in the morning but the goods do not cross to the other side until late morning or afternoon. This presents problems on the receiving side with negligible early morning workloads, but high afternoon demand often requires importers to pay substantial amounts of overtime. Cooperation between authorities on either side of the borders can help resolve this type of problem.

Customs Cooperation Committees

Article 12 of the WTO TFA concerns customs cooperation. It sets out the terms and requirements for members to share information to ensure effective customs control while respecting the confidentiality of the information exchanged. It allows flexibility in establishing the legal basis for information exchange. WTO members can enter into or maintain bilateral, plurilateral, or regional agreements for sharing or exchanging customs information and data, including advance information. The Revised Kyoto Convention in its general annex (standard 6.7) calls for cooperation between customs and for them to forge mutual administrative assistance agreements to enhance customs control. The WCO's SAFE Framework requires members to establish and enhance customs-to-customs network arrangements to promote the seamless movement of goods through secure international trade supply chains.

Customs cooperation is three-dimensional: cooperation with the trading community, between national customs authorities, and between customs and other border agencies. For the first, this has been mainly undertaken through the formation of national trade facilitation committees. While the primary function of these committees is to drive the implementation of the TFA, it has a wider remit of acting as a consultation medium with the broader trading community. In some BIMSTEC countries, these committees have evolved into national transport and trade facilitation committees with even wider remits. These committees should promote facilitation, study international trade and transport regulatory best practices, prepare recommendations, and foster transparency on important trade and transport initiatives. Such committees are normally serviced by a ministry as a secretariat, with leadership being provided by boards comprising of senior representatives of the business community and government. All the BIMSTEC countries have set up these committees. Sri Lanka and Myanmar each have a national trade facilitation committee, while India has its National Committee on Trade Facilitation. Despite the differing titles, their functions are broadly similar. Bangladesh, Bhutan, Nepal, and Thailand have national transport and trade facilitation committees.

The second form of customs cooperation is through regional cooperation mechanisms. SASEC's Customs Subgroup was set up in 2013 to "promote subregional trade facilitation initiatives through concerted customs reforms and modernization, strengthened inter-agency cooperation, and enhanced partnerships with the private sector to eliminate nontariff barriers to trade development."[11] It also discusses and agrees on action plans for the customs-related strategic thrusts under the SASEC Trade Facilitation Strategic Framework, and national and regional capacity-building programs for SASEC countries. SAARC has a working group on customs cooperation and ASEAN holds an annual meeting of the ASEAN director-generals of customs.

BIMSTEC has a custom working group, whose main function is to finalize the Agreement on Cooperation and Mutual Assistance in Customs Matters for the BIMSTEC Free Trade Area. This aims to promote customs cooperation within the region and is at the final draft stage. Creating a customs cooperation committee after the BIMSTEC Free Trade Area Agreement comes into force could be a consideration.

The third form of customs cooperation is with the other border agencies. The trade facilitation indicators of the OECD in Appendix II show that several BIMSTEC countries score poorly on internal customs cooperation. In practice, the border police or its equivalent is the lead agency for the movement of people and customs leads freight. When freight is moved using through-transport, there is an increased need for cooperation between the two for coordinated driver and freight clearance. But because of the low levels of through-transport in the BIMSTEC region, the two agencies tend to pursue separate roles. Cooperation between customs and other agencies involved in freight clearance at borders, such as sanitary and phytosanitary, tends to be closest. Cooperation at borders is often satisfactory, but less so at the national level. Only a few BIMSTEC countries have cooperation mechanisms specifically linking their border agencies, which come under the jurisdiction of different ministries. The further advancement of NSWs should promote increased cooperation between customs and these other border agencies.

Time-Release Studies

Time-release studies were established by the WCO as a tool to measure trade facilitation performance with the end goal of improving it. Data is collected on the time it takes for cargo to proceed through each clearance process from the time of the arrival of the mode of transportation at a border until the goods exit that airport, seaport, or road border. This is sometimes referred to as the border/seaport/airport dwell time. The collection of data is undertaken by customs staff at borders, as well as by other government agencies and private sector stakeholders. A challenge faced by BIMSTEC countries in conducting their own time-release studies is ensuring the data collected reflects the actual time taken to move the goods through the overall process. Another issue is identifying the inefficient processes that cause bottlenecks. Given these challenges, these studies are often undertaken using neutral external resources, including IFIs, UNESCAP, and the WCO.

---

[11] SASEC Discussion Platforms: Technical subcommittees: SASEC Customs Subgroup

The WCO's time-release study methodology measures the performance of customs activities as they directly relate to trade facilitation at borders. It not only evaluates aspects of the effectiveness of operational procedures at customs but also the performance of other agencies involved in clearances. The methodology also seeks to accurately measure the time elements of trade flows, thus allowing decisions to be made to improve performance.

Time-release studies can be an important benchmarking mechanism to help identify progress in implementing the strategic framework. These studies have been undertaken in all the BIMSTEC countries, but with an emphasis on land borders. The WCO model may need to be extended to seaports because of the increase in the number of parties involved. External technical assistance may also be needed to ensure the reliability of the data reported to the BIMSTEC's Secretariat or any institutional monitoring mechanism.

Customs Legislation

BIMSTEC countries have varying forms of legislation covering trade facilitation. For customs services, the general approach is a customs act setting out the role and responsibilities of customs. This is followed by subsidiary rules and regulations determining how the act is to be implemented. Customs acts can usually only be altered by parliament, whereas rules and regulations can be changed by ministries or by customs themselves. In general, rules and regulations are subject to regular alteration to reflect changes in practices and procedures. In some cases, these are included in acts, making them more comprehensive in scope.

Trade facilitation occurs in a dynamic environment requiring regular changes in practices and procedures and the adoption of advanced customs approaches with the increased use of automation. In general, these changes can be done by issuing new rules and regulations. But a problem arises when these advanced procedures cannot be implemented due to the provisions in the customs acts of the member states. Amending primary legislation is time-consuming because it needs inter-ministerial approval and endorsement by national cabinets before it can be put to parliaments, where it may then also be subject to further revisions. The time for parliamentary legislative debate is usually limited and subject to national priorities. Thus, changes in customs legislation have inherent extended lead times. The amended legislation also has to be compliant with member states' agreements with the WCO and WTO. The problem becomes more pronounced when amendments include secondary legislation.

Bangladesh's customs operate under the Customs Act of 1969, but a new act, tabled in 2018, is going through the approval process. Bhutan introduced a new Customs Act in 2017 and it is in the process of changing rules and regulations to be compliant with the Revised Kyoto Convention. India's Customs operate under the Customs Act of 1962. In Myanmar, customs are governed by the Sea Customs Act (1878, amended 2015), the Land Customs Act of 1924, the Export-Import Law of 2012, and the Tariff Law of 1992. Nepal's customs operate under the Nepal's Department of Customs Act 2064 (2007). In Thailand, the latest Customs Act was passed in 2017.

Some customs legislation needs updating, especially if old laws are a barrier to change. Anecdotal evidence suggests this is already the case in some BIMSTEC countries, especially for introducing risk management, AEO, post-auditing, and the automation of certain procedures including acceptance of digital signatures. Legislation may also not be compliant with the TFA. While amendments and secondary legislation, such as customs regulations, can address these aspects, updating primary legislation eliminates the potential problem of amendments not necessarily taking legal precedence over the original legislation. This situation has sometimes led to legal caveats that have been exploited by differing parties in some countries.

Mutual Recognition Agreements

BIMSTEC countries have only entered into a few mutual recognition agreements (MRAs) with each other. This is because the validity of tests and standards undertaken in one country is often not accepted by another. For example, sanitary or quality certificates from country A will not be accepted by country B without that country redoing the same tests on imports to provide national certification. In some countries, testing is required for every shipment, as opposed to type-approval certification. The lack of MRAs and the need for constant retesting is a significant NTB in the BIMSTEC region, especially for food and electrical products.

The strategic framework should promote discussion between BIMSTEC countries for promoting common standards wherever possible and assist in obtaining authorization for laboratories in neighboring countries to undertake approved testing on their behalf. The objective is that goods subject to testing in country A can be approved by certified testing in country B before export, which will help eliminate delays at the border awaiting country A to retest the product. Where this is not possible, conformance testing should be done to provide type-approval product certification rather than testing individual consignments.

If many more MRAs could be negotiated, it would be useful to establish protocols whereby the authorities in importing countries could access certifications online, to either clear goods in the absence of a required certificate or to check the validity of documents being produced by importers. This could also apply to certificates of origin, as well as for sanitary, phytosanitary, and trading standards certificates. In the absence of MRAs, the use of risk management by sanitary, phytosanitary, and technical barriers to trade agencies accepting test certificates by export countries could be used as an interim strategy.

Improving Hard Infrastructure

While resolving soft infrastructure constraints is critical, this needs to be supported by investments in complementary hard infrastructure—the facilities where the clearance processes and procedures are physically conducted. The extent of this infrastructure can have a direct impact on the efficiency of border and inland clearance of import and export trade. For soft infrastructure, the TFA can be applied as a basis for benchmarking and determining progress being made under the strategic framework. No international agreement, however, covers hard infrastructure because the nature and demands of these facilities vary significantly between BIMSTEC countries, and often even within a country.

Infrastructure developments by governments and in regional programs, such as ADB's GMS and SASEC initiatives and World Bank programs, are generally project-based. Progress is defined by the completion of or establishment of specific physical infrastructure, with national or strategic plans identifying potential projects whose realization would enhance trade facilitation directly or indirectly. Any similar BIMSTEC trade facilitation initiative would be expected to adopt a similar approach, and this was the methodology used in the BIMSTEC Master Plan for Transport Connectivity. The following sections highlight the types of infrastructure required and the likely challenges in their provision.

Land Border Infrastructure

Border crossings represent breaks in the international logistics chain. These disruptions occur not only because of the lack of through-transport but also the need to undertake complex clearance procedures. In many cases, the ownership of goods changes at borders, depending on the trading terms being used. While the application of modern practices and procedures as promoted by the Revised Kyoto Convention and the TFA can minimize these delays, having adequate infrastructure is vital for enabling the efficient performance of these more advanced procedures in a controlled environment. The modern trend is for facilities at land borders to merely serve as checkpoints for freight traffic, rather than as final clearance points.

This can be achieved by pre-clearing exports before they arrive at borders, with authorities at frontiers simply checking the paperwork and, if necessary, doing a visual inspection of the vehicle. This strategy has already been adopted by some BIMSTEC countries. The process is similar for imports. Here, the inward paperwork is checked, the vehicle and cargo inspected, and the shipment is allowed to proceed inland with transit documents to a point where it is finally cleared. Dwell times within border control points are minimized. These control points have simple layouts, consisting of separate lanes for passenger and freight traffic with processing booths and adjacent administrative offices.

Unfortunately, this approach has been difficult to implement in the BIMSTEC region and, indeed, in many other developing countries for a variety of reasons. Apart from the lack of through-transport, current practices and procedures combined with typically large numbers of small traders mean that most border posts continue to act as final clearance facilities with high levels of examination, thus requiring more substantial border facilities. In some cases, border facilities act as actual clearance points; in others, a supporting land port has been built nearby for the final cargo clearance of goods.

Through-transport is permitted between India and Nepal, but with time limits for return transport to the country of origin. Through-transport between India and Bhutan is permitted, but with significant restrictions due to the lower weight and axle loads requirements in Bhutan because of its mountainous terrain. No through-transport exists between India and Bangladesh, India and Myanmar, Bangladesh and Myanmar, Bangladesh and Bhutan/Nepal, and Thailand and Myanmar other than local vehicles and those taking or collecting from border facilities on the other side. The Bangladesh, Bhutan, India, and Nepal Motor Vehicles Agreement has been signed by all countries, except Bhutan. Its main benefit will likely be between India and Bangladesh. After some delays, discussions are underway to agree on a memorandum of understanding to implement the agreement. For freight, this will only cover containerized movements. There are concerns, particularly in Bangladesh, that it will favor the larger Indian operators. It is proposed that ICDs are used to help operationalize the implementation of the agreement. This could turn out to be similar to the Greater Mekong Subregion Cross-Border Agreement, where the main advantages were initially for passenger vehicles (buses) rather than freight transport.

Investment in border infrastructure has been the centerpiece of trade facilitation efforts in many of the BIMSTEC countries in recent years. The Government of India has an ongoing program for building integrated check posts (ICPs) at its borders with Bangladesh, Myanmar, and Nepal, and it has set up ICPs at Petrapole, Agartala, Jogbani, Raxaul, and Moreh, all of which are already in operation. In Nepal, the investment by India covers both sides of the border, but in Bangladesh and Myanmar, it covers only the Indian side. Nepal opened an ICP at Birgunj (Sirsiya) in 2018 and Biratnagar in January 2020, as well as a land customs station at Karkarvitta. An ICP is planned at Bhairahawa, and an ICP at the Nepalgunj border is being built. Bangladesh is upgrading its border facility at Benapole and has established supporting land ports at the other main borders with India, some operated by the private sector. India has an extensive program to construct 13 new ICPs on the Indian side of the border, 7 with Bangladesh, 5 with Nepal, and 1 with Bhutan. The new Mae Sot-Myawaddy border crossing for freight traffic built by Myanmar and Thailand opened in October 2019. Bhutan plans a new border complex near Phuentsholing at Tolibari and is improving several secondary border crossings in the east of the country.

The design of these new border facilities generally complies with international best practices for separating inbound from outbound freight traffic, trucks from passenger cars, and buses from pedestrian traffic. Building new border facilities that bypass towns have in some cases resulted in the original border post being dedicated for pedestrian and car/bus traffic and freight using the new crossing point. A concern in some cases is that these new freight facilities may be too extensive, with designs being based on accommodating delays incurred under previous processing regimes. The danger is that these facilities merely move the queuing from adjacent border roads to the border control zone without any significant improvements in overall performance to justify the investment. Another concern is that some designs are not based on form-follows-function concepts but are based on standard designs, whereby the functions have to be fitted into the layout rather than vice versa. Different borders have differing requirements and applying standard designs can lead to overinvestment with large sprawling layouts. This can result in staffing problems, particularly as many BIMSTEC borders tend to be far from large conurbations. Overcapacity is often manifested by vacant booths or unused processing points due to the lack of personnel or demand, and the long distances between individual checking points and processing offices.

Another challenge in border investment is that border processing tends to become progressively devolved as trade demand increases. This is because the origins and destinations of trade expand beyond the primary population centers. Stakeholders want more secondary borders to be upgraded rather than having to incur additional transport costs traveling farther to use the primary border crossings. Thus, the need for further investment in smaller border facilities is an ongoing challenge, particularly along the border between India and Bangladesh, India and Nepal, and India and Bhutan. The terrain in Myanmar will likely limit the number of border crossings with its BIMSTEC neighbors.

Inland Clearance Depots

The concept of land border checkpoints followed by final clearance inland may be difficult to realize in the near term due to transit risks, but this is not necessarily the case for container traffic. Containers with imports can be sealed at seaports and then transported to ICDs located closer to the importer or end-user. This practice not only makes clearance easier but also enables inbound containers to move more rapidly through ports, rather than congesting container terminals while awaiting clearance. As trade expands, pressure will mount on the main BIMSTEC seaports to increase the percentage of containers being cleared outside the port areas. The primary role of an ICD is to act as an extension of the seaport container yard—that is, away from the port and closer to the main points of import demand or, in some cases, export demand. Dwell times in many BIMSTEC ports remain high by international comparison and the demand to move more containers faster through the seaports is growing as a sustainable method to reduce congestion at the maritime interface.

India has already established a national network of ICDs, estimated at over 80. Many of them are served by rail as well as road, with the Container Corporation of India Ltd operating over 50 facilities and running block trains between their ICDs and seaports. Bangladesh has a large ICD in Kamalapur, Dhaka, which is linked to Chattogram (Chittagong) port by rail. Bhutan has recently built the dry port in Phuentsholing acting as an ICD, with another to be completed at Tolibari. Nepal has an ICD at Birgunj (Sirsiya) linked by road and rail to the seaports of Kolkata, Haldia, and Visakhapatnam. Thailand has the large Lat Krabang ICD in eastern Bangkok linked to Laem Chabang seaport and ICDs at Chiang Rai and Natha.

Additional ICD capacity will be required to avoid increased congestion and to support the faster clearance of container traffic. Dhaka's ICD had a 14% increase in traffic in 2019 to 95,000 twenty-foot equivalent units and is almost at capacity. A second ICD near Dhirasram railway station has been under discussion for some years and appears to be reaching finalization with DP Ports indicating their possible involvement on a PPP basis. Myanmar has several ICDs in Yangon and is planning two more, one at Mandalay. Nepal has completed the construction of an ICD at Chobhar, Kathmandu, which is expected to start operations soon. In Sri Lanka, a decision has been taken by the government to relocate the containerized inspection activities carried out in Colombo to Kerawalapitiya to avoid congestion, as well as to improve efficiency and capacity. Containerized cargo inspection is currently being done at three privately-owned yards located close to Colombo Port. The Cabinet of Ministers has approved the allocation of the relevant land for this purpose and has taken steps to set up the proposed inspection center with state-of-art technologies. The ongoing financial crisis in the country would be expected to delay implementation. India has an ICD at Siliguri that has potential benefits for trade with Bhutan and eastern Nepal.

Land Ports

The concept of simple border checks at land borders, followed by inland clearance, will inevitably take time to fully operationalize, mainly because of the lack of through-transport arrangements and secure inland transport transit regimes for non-containerized cargoes. Consequently, border clearance facilities need to be established, either within the border control zones or in their immediate vicinity. As a way to reduce congestion at borders, land ports provide a supporting role to land borders similar to the role of ICDs in supporting seaports. Land ports are normally located close to border posts, thus eliminating the need for transit regimes.

The main function of land ports is to clear import and export freight moving by road through the adjacent border posts and to provide transshipment services where through-transport is not permitted. In some cases, facilities are still located within the overall border control zones, but in other instances, they can be several kilometers "inland." Building land ports can alleviate the need for large complexes, such as ICPs at the physical borders.

Bangladesh has 23 land ports of which Akhaura, Benapole, Bhomra, Burimari, and Nakugaon are operated by the Bangladesh Land Ports Authority, and Banglabandha, Bibirbazar, Hili, Sonamosjid, Hili, and Teknaf by private operators on a build-operate-transfer basis. A private port operator has been appointed to construct and operate Birol land port with the remaining 12 land ports (Balla, Belonia, Chilahati, Darshana Daulatgan, Dhanua Kamalpur, Gobrakura-Koroitoli, Ramgarh, Sheola, Sonahat, Tamabil Tegamukh) under development. Nepal has dry ports at Biratnagar, Bhairahawa, Kararbhitta, and Tatopini on the PRC border. Bhutan has a single dry port at Phuentsholing and a nominal ICD at Tolibari will eventually become a land port. Myanmar has two land ports, at least nominally, one at

Myitnge (Mandalay) and Ywa Thargyi (Yangon); the former would normally be classified as an ICD because it is not at a border. Thailand is planning a land port at Udon Thani on the border with the Lao People's Democratic Republic.

Container Freight Stations

A Container Freight Station (CFS) is a facility where freight is consolidated (grouped) or deconsolidated (separated) at the container interface between the land and maritime transport modes. CFSs were originally established inside ports to handle less-than-containerload traffic, often using the excess port labor resulting from the transition from conventional general cargo to container handling. This role has extended to stuffing and de-stuffing full containerload traffic where inland transportation in containerized form is not possible due to road, bridge, or customer access restrictions. CFSs have gradually been established outside seaports as terminal yards have become more congested and ports have less excess labor. CFSs effectively have a similar role to land ports by supporting maritime borders in handling the clearance of containers at an adjacent location. Border authorities are located at CFSs, just as they are at ICDs and land ports.

All India's largest seaports have supporting off-dock CFSs that are used for both less-than-containerload and full containerload traffic. In some cases, they are also used for full containerload movements that are delivered later still within the container to the receiver. In this case, the CFSs provide temporary storage as a direct extension of port terminals. In Bangladesh off-dock CFSs have been permitted since 2016, but there are only a few at Chattogram and most CFS activity is still within the port area. Sri Lanka has six off-dock CFSs, although CFS operations continue at locations within the port itself. Yangon has had CFSs in the industrial port and off-dock CFSs since 2014. Many of Myanmar's CFS developments have been in the Dagon district near Highway 1. Thailand has both on-dock and off-dock CFSs.

The trend in many developed countries has been to gradually phase out on-dock CFSs to reduce warehousing inside the port to free up open space for container handling and storage. BIMSTEC seaports will likely follow this trend, and so promoting off-dock CFS terminals will become increasingly important. Evidence suggests that less-than-containerload shipments may significantly increase due to changing trading practices, such as e-commerce and just-in-time shipping. CFSs are intended to be able to process this extra demand.

Testing Stations and Laboratories

All border agencies need facilities to test certain products being traded through their borders. This is to validate the products being declared, ensure they meet standards in recipient countries, and identify illicit goods and false documentation. Immigration and border police have generally adequate testing equipment for checking identity documentation. However, customs at most borders only have rudimentary testing equipment and mini-laboratories on-site to check for illicit material and these often lack the technical expertise or chemicals to undertake complex testing. Few of the other border agencies such as sanitary, phytosanitary, and trading standards have testing facilities located at the border and rely on sending samples away for testing to central laboratories. Because most BIMSTEC land borders are far from large cities, this can result in significant delays in obtaining test results. Surveys show the chief cause of extended delays in clearances at borders is often caused by testing delays.

This raises two important aspects. The first is the approval of agencies in, say, country A to do testing and certification on behalf of country B. For example, government or private laboratories in Nepal undertake testing and certification of India-bound products to the standard required by the Indian authorities and vice versa. A problem is that laboratories in some BIMSTEC countries do not meet international standards, and so the potential for accreditation and promoting MRAs becomes limited. The second is the lack of laboratories close to land border posts, including the main ones. This results in delays when a product is dispatched from the border to city laboratories, tested, certified, and the results sent back. If it is not possible to set up more laboratories due to resource constraints (technical, financial, or staffing), it will be important to install online certification methodologies so that test certificates can be issued online at border posts to enable the speedy release of shipments.

Changes in Trade Logistics

Advanced logistics in most BIMSTEC countries continue to lag behind global standards. This is cited as a likely cause of the relatively low performance of these countries in the World Bank's Logistics Performance Index. External pressures will result in changes in the way international trade is conducted and it is vital that trade facilitation in the BIMSTEC region is capable of responding positively to these changes, thereby avoiding new NTBs from emerging.

GVCs already exist in BIMSTEC countries to a greater or lesser extent. The location of links along these chains is determined by many factors, including technical expertise, wage levels, taxation, capital development costs, transport charges, access and reliability, and ease of moving products internationally to and from the different processes within the GVC (i.e., the relevant trade facilitation). COVID-19 has triggered a situation in which firms are actively re-evaluating their current GVC arrangements.

Pressure is increasing for made-at-home production to eliminate trade-war risks and utilizing a possible unemployment "bubble" caused by the economic impact of the COVID-19 pandemic. This 'bubble' has proved transitory in many developed countries with a rapid transition to lower unemployment levels as restrictions have been lifted. However, this is not the case in many developing countries. BIMSTEC countries are well placed to attract more GVC activity, especially from East Asia, but to do this they will need to have efficient trade facilitation practices to ensure that products can move rapidly and reliably through their borders and seaports.

Against this backdrop, reliability in international logistics is expected to become far more important. Supply chain management involving the movement and storage of raw materials, work-in-progress inventories, and finished goods from point of origin to point of consumption will become more common in developing country regions, like BIMSTEC. This will include new systems with tracking and tracing capabilities, and shipment visibility, such that the supply chain becomes more transparent, highlighting any delays incurred at borders and ports.

Vendor-managed inventory services are also expected to increase. Here, the buyer of a product provides certain information to the supplier (vendor) of that product and the supplier takes full responsibility for maintaining an agreed inventory of the material, usually at the buyer's consumption location. Vendor-managed inventory operations are designed to meet the demand for new business models and attract investments, especially in higher value-added manufacturing. This is likely to create increased demand for bonded storage premises and, possibly, for more post-auditing.

E-commerce has been one of the beneficiaries of the COVID-19 pandemic, both nationally and internationally. The rise in e-commerce has not only increased traffic passing through international mail centers, airport transit sheds, and courier terminals but also created the need for faster clearance of goods regardless of how they are transported. Anecdotal evidence suggests that e-commerce and e-trade are now well established and set to expand their market shares. This will warrant enhancing soft infrastructure to ensure expedited clearances.

The foremost seaports are gradually expanding their use of advanced ICT systems. Most BIMSTEC ports have installed some form of terminal operating system and container terminal management system, often by the terminal operators introducing these systems as part of their concession arrangements. The next step is establishing port community systems (PCSs) linking all the members of the port communities. In this respect, they are similar to NSWs, which link members of the trade facilitation community. PCSs connect the diverse parties involved in seaport activities through a neutral and open electronic platform. This enables a secure exchange of information between public and private stakeholders, thereby improving the competitive position of seaport communities. PCSs optimize, manage, and automate port- and logistics-efficient processes through the single submission of data and connect transport and logistics chains.

PCSs facilitate the exchange of data between parties and give access in real-time to the status of consignments as they undergo the various processes between the arrival of goods at the ports by sea in the case of imports and transshipments and their exit by either sea or land and vice versa for exports. It is vital that customs' IT systems or NSWs can interface with PCSs since trade facilitation is a critical element in the efficiency of port logistics. India has recently developed a national PCS, Bangladesh has a PCS at Chattogram, and HPC Hamburg Port Consulting GmbH has been awarded a contract to establish a PCS for Thailand. Myanmar and Sri Lanka are actively planning their PCSs.

The key to adapting to these various logistical developments is awareness, that those involved in trade facilitation understand the external changes in trading practices and activities likely to affect their environment. This will enable the advancement of both soft and hard infrastructure to accommodate the nature of future demands in a proactive rather than reactive manner. Singapore, for one, has built a reputation for being abreast with changes in trading and logistics practices and being responsive to the needs of the trading community. This highlights the importance of having an effective communication medium between the trade and transport community and the entities responsible for trade facilitation, particularly customs.

Institution and Capacity Building

The trade facilitation demands of the trading community over the next 10 years will change significantly, as will the responses to these changes by border agencies. The latter will be determined by the wider application of advanced processing and procedures, supported by even higher levels of automation. The traditional roles and working practices of customs officers and other border officials will likely alter appreciably. But the exact nature and timing of these changes are difficult to predict, other than by possibly using the experience of countries with the most advanced trade facilitation.

Change inherently raises the need for institutional and capacity-building programs such that new approaches to processing and procedures can be implemented. This will involve not only technical training but also changes in mindsets and trust. Anecdotal evidence suggests that automation in some countries has been held back because border agency officers have not completely bought into these new approaches, resulting in automated and manual systems running in parallel. The change will likely be particularly difficult at the more remote land border posts and land ports.

Trade facilitation in the BIMSTEC region varies significantly. Thailand and India are more advanced; Bangladesh and Sri Lanka are in transition; and Bhutan, Myanmar, and Nepal have the least developed trade facilitation environments, although both are making significant progress. The appreciable differences in their trade facilitation situations will require an approach that reflects this in their institutional and capacity-building needs. This suggests that a more holistic approach is needed to identify the overall needs for capacity building, without specifying in which particular area it is needed.

The differing development situation in the BIMSTEC countries can be an advantage rather than a constraint. BIMSTEC's more advanced economies could provide capacity-building assistance to the less advanced ones by providing training and skill transfer initiatives. IFIs including ADB, USAID, the World Bank, the WCO, and WTO could also act as resource providers, particularly for advancing soft infrastructure and technical training. These international organizations are already assisting some BIMSTEC countries to upgrade their customs computer systems and develop NSWs and trade information portals. Such external assistance requires compatible internal institutional and capacity building to ensure these applications are not only implemented successfully but also become self-sustaining. Without support for training, making progress will be more difficult and investment in soft infrastructure could be put at risk. Most BIMSTEC countries are well aware of the need for initiatives to build this capacity. In some cases, however, trainers to conduct programs equipped with the appropriate knowledge and skills may not be there to implement these new techniques or technical initiatives. To overcome this, Thailand and India, as well as other countries that have this expertise, could be brought in to help.

Customs officers need new skill sets, particularly those linked to the inevitable increase in ICT. Trained personnel in specialist areas must be retained within the service. There are concerns that staff rotation policies and government service remuneration levels in some BIMSTEC countries risk the loss of key trained personnel. Indeed, some countries already have significant staff turnover, and these losses are a particular problem with ICT personnel as they have skills sought by the private sector. Staff retention will become an increasingly important focus in capacity-building programs. The overall goal is to raise the professionalism and status of personnel engaged in trade facilitation, whereby improved performance is reflected in better pay and lower staff turnover.

Another important area of cooperation between the BIMSTEC countries could be promoting a knowledge-sharing platform to exchange intelligence, such as on smuggling and other risk-related aspects. Such intelligence is usually exchanged on a bilateral basis, but wider circulation on a regional basis could be beneficial, provided that the confidentiality issues can be adequately addressed.

STRUCTURE, CONTENT, AND MONITORING MECHANISMS OF THE STRATEGIC FRAMEWORK

This section discusses the structure, content, and monitoring mechanisms of the strategic framework. While various structures could be adopted, it is important that the framework's contents are compatible with the trade facilitation strategies that member states have endorsed as participants in other regional groupings. These regional groupings and their membership are as follows (BIMSTEC countries in italics):

- ASEAN: Brunei Darussalam, Cambodia, Indonesia, Lao PDR, Malaysia, *Myanmar*, Philippines, Singapore, Timor-Leste, *Thailand*, and Viet Nam;
- Ayeyawady-Chao Phraya-Mekong Economic Cooperation Strategy— Cambodia, Lao PDR, *Myanmar, Thailand*, and Viet Nam;
- GMS: Cambodia, Lao PDR, *Myanmar,* PRC (specifically Yunnan Province and Guangxi Zhuang Autonomous Region), *Thailand*, and Viet Nam;
- SAARC: Afghanistan, *Bangladesh, Bhutan, India*, Maldives, *Nepal,* Pakistan, and *Sri Lanka;* and
- SASEC: *Bangladesh, Bhutan, India*, Maldives, *Myanmar, Nepal, and Sri Lanka.*

SASEC's membership is the closest to BIMSTEC's membership, with Thailand being the only non-member. SAARC has all but two (Myanmar and Thailand) BIMSTEC members. ASEAN, the Ayeyawady-Chao Phraya-Mekong Economic Cooperation Strategy, and the GMS do not include five BIMSTEC members. This indicates that compatibility with SASEC's trade facilitation strategies is probably the most important for BIMSTEC, while also taking Thailand's situation into account.

Structure of Regional Strategic Plans

The framework structure used in other strategic planning initiatives under SASEC and BIMSTEC programs is discussed in the following subsections, based on the order of their publication. This is followed by the proposed structure for the strategic framework.

South Asia Subregional Economic Cooperation Trade Facilitation Strategic Framework 2014–2018

This initiative grew out of a SASEC Trade Facilitation Week held in March 2013 that identified the need to prepare, formulate, and implement a strategy and roadmap for reforming and modernizing trade facilitation in the SASEC subregion, particularly focusing on customs. This was in response to the bottlenecks in trade facilitation being identified as the leading NTBs in the subregion, and the low rankings of SASEC countries in the World Bank's Doing Business surveys and Logistics Performance Index. Despite some notable progress in implementing SASEC's strategic framework, some residual constraints remain.

The structure of the 20-page SASEC Trade Facilitation Strategic Framework 2014–2018 was initially based on a four-tier logical sequence, starting with a mission statement defining the framework's overarching objective[12]. This was followed by the overall strategic goals being identified, indicating what the framework's contents intended to achieve and how progress on realizing those goals could be measured. The scope of the plan was then divided into individual components or areas of interest that the framework sought to address. Each component was then subdivided into a series of strategic thrusts, each identifying actions to be undertaken to achieve the preset goals, and hence fulfill the overall mission. This structure is shown in Figure 4 below.

An analysis of the text in the published framework document indicates there were some minor deviations from the initial structure shown below. The framework (footnote 11) states the overall mission as being to "promote the prosperity of the subregion by facilitating the efficient movement of trade across borders" and the goal for trade facilitation was to "increase intraregional trade through increased interregional trade facilitation efficiency and a reduction in the time and cost to trade." The strategy was defined as elevating the "practice and process of border standards to international standards and international best practices, including automation." The priority areas (components) continued to be the same as those shown in Figure 4, but also included institution

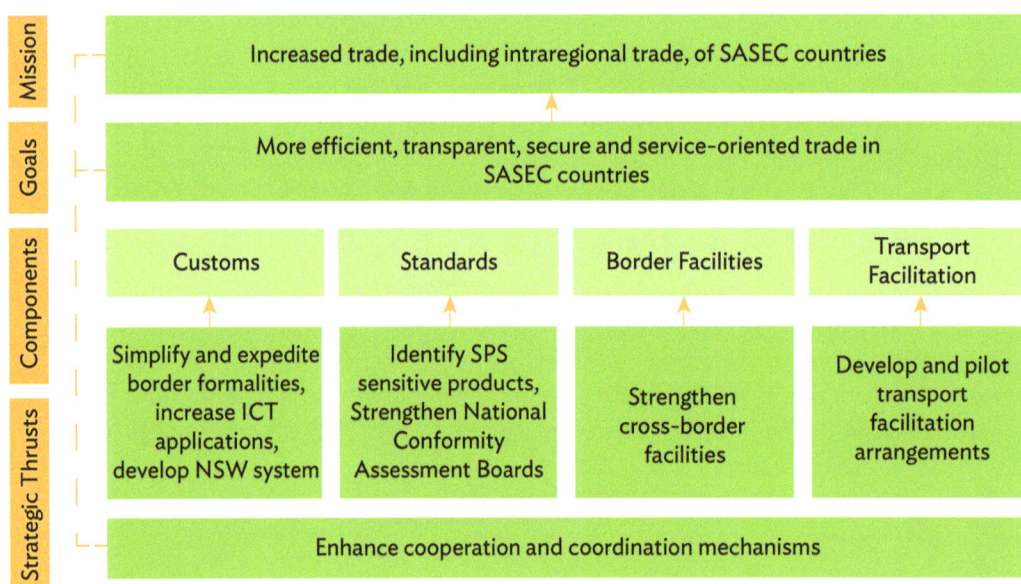

Figure 4: Initial Structure of the South Asia Subregional Economic Cooperation Trade Facilitation Strategic Framework, 2014–2018

Mission	Increased trade, including intraregional trade, of SASEC countries
Goals	More efficient, transparent, secure and service-oriented trade in SASEC countries
Components	Customs · Standards · Border Facilities · Transport Facilitation
Strategic Thrusts	Simplify and expedite border formalities, increase ICT applications, develop NSW system · Identify SPS sensitive products, Strengthen National Conformity Assessment Boards · Strengthen cross-border facilities · Develop and pilot transport facilitation arrangements
	Enhance cooperation and coordination mechanisms

ICT = information and communication technology, NSW = national single window, SASEC = South Asia Subregional Economic Cooperation, SPS = sanitary and phytosanitary.
Source: Asian Development Bank. 2014: SASEC Trade Facilitation Strategic Framework 2014-2018. Manila.

---

[12]   South Asian Subregional Economic Cooperation and Asian Development Bank. 2014. *South Asia Subregional Economic Cooperation: Trade Facilitation Strategic Framework 2014–2018*. October. Manila. https://www.adb.org/publications/sasec-trade-facilitation-strategic-framework-2014-2018.

and capacity building. These were then broken down into strategic thrusts that when combined would achieve the overall strategy.

This suggests that a five-tier structure was finally adopted: mission, goal, strategy, components, and strategic thrusts. This was mainly due to the insertion of an upper-level mission, whereby the original mission shown in Figure 4 became a goal and that goal became a strategy. It will be important for BIMSTEC to clearly define the purpose of each level in its strategic framework to avoid possible duplication or loss of focus.

South Asia Subregional Economic Cooperation Operational Plan 2016–2025

In 2016, SASEC, in pursuit of transport, trade facilitation, and energy linkages, identified the need for a comprehensive long-term plan to build on its achievements since 2001. The SASEC Operational Plan 2016–2025 defined its strategic objectives for transport, energy, and trade facilitation, and added a focus on corridor development. Each strategic objective was linked to well-defined operational priorities, supported by a long list of individual projects identified by SASEC member countries.

The structure of this 45-page SASEC Operational Plan 2016–2025[13] has similarities with the 2014–2018 strategic framework in which an overarching SASEC goal or mission statement was inserted to "increase trade and economic cooperation within South Asia, create links to East and Southeast Asia and promote sustainable and inclusive economic growth through regional cooperation." The more specific mission for trade facilitation was the adoption of a "comprehensive approach to transport and trade facilitation, expanding the focus from land-based to sea-borne investments in multimodal networks." The specific objective or goal for trade facilitation was to "make cross-border trade and transport in the subregion faster, cheaper, and more predictable, while maintaining the security of the supply chain and ensuring the effectiveness and efficiency of the institutions involved."

Unlike the structure of the trade facilitation strategic framework, the operational priorities or components were transport, trade facilitation, and energy—that is, they were sector- rather than subject-based due to their wider remits. Within each of these sector components were sub-components and operational priorities (strategic thrusts). The operational priorities were more comprehensive than those in the framework, despite this being only one of the four sectors to be addressed in the operational plan. These strategic thrusts were then iterated in 25 sub-operational priorities that set out how they should be implemented.

The operational plan has six tiers—mission, components, sub-mission, sub-goals, sub-components, and strategic thrusts. The chief difference between the structure of the operational plan and the strategic framework was the need for additional levels due to the plan's wider scope.

---

[13]   Asian Development Bank. 2016. *South Asa Subregional Economic Cooperation: Operational Plan 2016–2025*. September. Manila. https://www.adb.org/documents/sasec-operational-plan-2016-2025.

Association of Southeast Asian Nations Trade Facilitation Framework and Strategic Action Plan

The 2017 ASEAN Trade Facilitation Framework was aimed at consolidating the trade facilitation elements in various ASEAN plans, together with those of the WCO and WTO. It was designed to provide a basis on which ASEAN member states could further engage in and foster greater trade facilitation regionally and within ASEAN sectoral bodies. The ASEAN Trade Facilitation Framework focused on implementing ASEAN obligations, commitments, and instruments for trade facilitation.

The framework is a compact 5-page policy document setting out the guidelines for developing and implementing a comprehensive ASEAN trade facilitation work program geared to achieve specific and measurable deliverables. It consists of four sections addressing the program's scope, objectives, principles, and implementation. The defined scope was to cover customs and transport facilitation, transparency of trade regulations and procedures, standards and conformance, private sector engagement, and business facilitation. The objectives section cited seven goals, and the principles section provided guidance and direction for further developing and implementing the program with 10 components. The implementation section identified how the framework was to be carried out, with the first element being to establish a strategic action plan.

The ASEAN Trade Facilitation Strategic Action Plan is the more relevant document for comparative purposes than the overarching ASEAN Trade Facilitation Framework[14]. This again is a compact 9-page document with four main structural components—vision, mission, goals, and strategic objectives. The strategic objectives were then broken down into actions, outputs, outcomes, outcome indicators, timelines, and responsible bodies for implementation. The seven strategic objectives were:

- Encouraging the accelerated implementation of trade facilitation measures, which have been accepted by international institutions, such as the WTO and/or the WCO, and in light of other best practices;
- Achieving the competitive, efficient, and seamless movement of goods within the Southeast Asian region to enhance ASEAN's trade and production networks, better participate in global value chains, and establish a highly integrated and cohesive economy;
- Establishing an effective and responsive regional approach to tackle the trade-distorting effects of NTB measures with a view to pursuing policy objectives while reducing the cost and time of doing business in ASEAN;
- Actively engaging the private sector, with particular emphasis on the development and promotion of micro, small, and medium-sized enterprises in the process of regional economic integration;
- Enhancing institutional coordination among ASEAN sectoral bodies to implement trade facilitation measures under their purview in a way that is consistent with their sector work plans for 2016–2025 and the ASEAN Blueprint 2025;
- Working toward increasing the participation of all ASEAN member states, especially the least developed ones, in implementing ASEAN trade facilitation programs; and

---

[14]   Association of Southeast Asian Nations. 2017. *AEC Trade Facilitation Strategic Action Plan.* Jakarta, Indonesia. https://asean.org/wp-content/uploads/2020/12/Adopted-AEC-2025-Trade-Facilitation-Strategic-Action-Plan-ATF-SAP.pdf.

- Improving the monitoring mechanism for the implementation of trade facilitation measures to increase their effectiveness and responsiveness in improving the competitiveness of ASEAN industries and businesses.

The strategic objectives demonstrate ASEAN's focus on the "new generation" definition of trade facilitation by citing the time and cost of trade, global value chains, active involvement of the private sector, and emphasizing the need for effective monitoring.

BIMSTEC Master Plan for Transport Connectivity

This was elaborated during 2018–2019 to be a strategic document to guide actions and promote synergy among the various regional frameworks to achieve enhanced connectivity and sustainable development in the BIMSTEC region. The document presents a comprehensive 10-year strategy and action plan for the region's transport connectivity, including trade facilitation. The structure shown in Figure 5 is similar to the plans discussed previously, except it has an upper-level overall BIMSTEC vision statement followed by strategic objectives relating to this vision. The master plan has its own specific vision statement. This structure broadly compares with SASEC's operational plan, which also addressed several subjects, rather than trade facilitation in isolation.

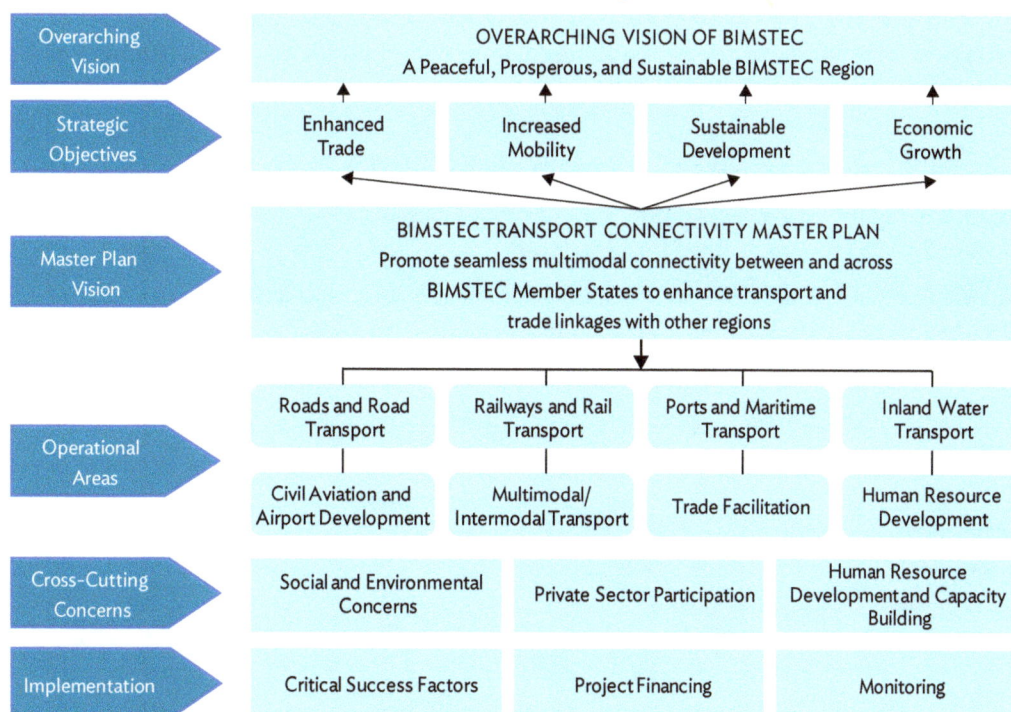

Figure 5: Building Blocks of the Master Plan for Transport Connectivity in the BIMSTEC Region

Overarching Vision	OVERARCHING VISION OF BIMSTEC A Peaceful, Prosperous, and Sustainable BIMSTEC Region
Strategic Objectives	Enhanced Trade / Increased Mobility / Sustainable Development / Economic Growth
Master Plan Vision	BIMSTEC TRANSPORT CONNECTIVITY MASTER PLAN Promote seamless multimodal connectivity between and across BIMSTEC Member States to enhance transport and trade linkages with other regions
Operational Areas	Roads and Road Transport / Railways and Rail Transport / Ports and Maritime Transport / Inland Water Transport / Civil Aviation and Airport Development / Multimodal/Intermodal Transport / Trade Facilitation / Human Resource Development
Cross-Cutting Concerns	Social and Environmental Concerns / Private Sector Participation / Human Resource Development and Capacity Building
Implementation	Critical Success Factors / Project Financing / Monitoring

BIMSTEC Bay of Bengal Initiative for Multi-Sectoral Technical and Economic Cooperation.
Source: Asian Development Bank. 2020. *BIMSTEC Master Plan for Transport Connectivity*. Manila (unpublished).

The masterplan differs from the strategic framework in that there are no goals specific to the vision since these are subsumed into each of the components or operational areas. Similar to SASEC's operational plan, the components are sector-based. The trade facilitation component is then divided into the following subcomponents:

- developing border infrastructure and facilities;
- developing ICDs;
- simplifying and harmonizing import, export, and transit documentation;
- further developing automated clearance systems;
- advanced logistics; and
- capacity-building in trade facilitation (contained in the human resources development component).

These subcomponents or operational areas were then subdivided into formulated policies and strategies. These policies represent the goals of the sub-components and strategic thrusts and indicate how these policies are to be achieved. Each sub-component has an implementation plan based on projects which could also be used as a monitoring mechanism. The master plan had an eight-tier structure—overall vision, strategic objectives, vision, components (operational areas), sub-components, policies, strategies, and projects—reflecting its wider remit.

Structure of BIMSTEC Trade Facilitation Strategic Framework 2030

Although the planning documents just discussed differ, they also have common elements. The SASEC Operational Plan and BIMSTEC Master Plan for Transport Connectivity cover several subjects (components), thus creating the need for additional layers within their planning structure. Table 6 shows the structural frameworks used in these planning documents.

Table 6: Structure of Plans Covering Trade Facilitation in the BIMSTEC Region

Structure	SASEC Trade Facilitation Framework	SASEC Operational Plan	ASEAN Trade Facilitation Action Plan	BIMSTEC Transport Connectivity Masterplan
Program mission/vision		X	X	X
Strategic objectives		X		X
Mission/vision	X	X	X	X
Goal	X	X	X	
Strategy	X			
Operational priorities/components	X	X		X
Subcomponents				X
Strategic thrusts	X	X	X	
Policies				X
Strategies		X		X
Projects		X		X

ASEAN = Association of Southeast Asian Nations, BIMSTEC = Bay of Bengal Initiative for Multi-Sectoral Technical and Economic Cooperation, SASEC = South Asia Subregional Economic Cooperation.

Source: Asian Development Bank.

It is important to differentiate this BIMSTEC strategic framework from these other regional initiatives. This can be done through its contents rather than by adopting a different structure. The framework's proposed structure incorporates the following structural elements from other plans:

- Overarching vision statement—links the framework to BIMSTEC's overall vision, thus providing *context*;
- Vision statement—defines *what* the framework is expected to accomplish and *why*;
- Mission statement—identifies *how* the vision will be achieved and is action-based;
- Strategic statement—indicates the *methods* to be used to undertake the mission;
- Goal—identifies what needs *to be accomplished* to realize the strategy and be able to monitor progress being achieved;
- Components and subcomponents—defines the *areas to be addressed* under the framework; and
- Sub-strategies and subgoals—identify how each subcomponent will be addressed to make progress on achieving subcomponent goals leading to *achieving the overall goal*.

This standard seven-tier linked framework structure has a combination of top-down and bottom-up approaches. For example, the vision of *what* and *why* cascades down to the mission of *how* to achieve the strategy, which in turn indicates the *way* towards achieving the goal that identifies the projected results. In the lower half of the structure, the implementation of sub-strategies and goals flow upward, culminating in achieving the overall goal and hence fulfilling the strategy, mission, and vision statements. Setting realistic, implementable, and measurable goals will be the most critical element of the strategic framework.

In addition to this structure, supporting cross-cutting components need to be included. These include the guiding principles to formulate the strategic framework, the mobilization of resources for its implementation, the monitoring mechanisms to identify progress being made to achieving the projected goals, and the cooperation and institutional mechanisms to manage the initiative.

The strategic framework needs to differentiate itself in two aspects from the other trade facilitation plans covering other parts of the Asian region. Firstly, its scope should incorporate the wider interpretations of trade facilitation. Secondly, it should be compatible with the other trade facilitation plans in the region without necessarily replicating or merely being the sum of their contents. Still, similarities in scope, both in the subject and the countries, mean that some level of duplication is inevitable. The ASEAN Trade Facilitation Framework is essentially a policy document that adopts a high-level approach by setting an overarching strategy that is then articulated in more detail in its Economic Community 2025 Trade Facilitation Action Plan. SASEC adopted a similar strategy with its initial higher-level overarching strategic framework that was followed later by a more detailed action plan setting out its implementation. The BIMSTEC Master Plan for Transport Connectivity is a high-level strategic planning document in which trade facilitation was only one component. This inevitably limited its coverage to just a few aspects.

This strategic framework is designed to address the overarching strategic aspects, as well as have a more operational flavor. The strategy is driven by the operational demands needed to enhance the region's trade facilitation. It extends the overarching SASEC and ASEAN trade facilitation approach by also including elements of their action plans, thus avoiding delays inherent in adopting a two-step process. This strategic framework does not go as far as detailing individual projects, but it indicates operational priorities that would normally be articulated in an action plan. Thus, it has greater coverage than previous regional frameworks, but less than those contained in a strategic framework–action plan combination.

Strategic Framework Components

The components and challenges in Section 5.1 vary according to their remit. In the case of both the SASEC Action Plan and the BIMSTEC Master Plan for Transport Connectivity, trade facilitation was only part of their scope. The action plan also addressed transport and energy; the master plan was predominantly oriented toward transport because of its transport connectivity remit. Nevertheless, all these plans raise some of the constraints as shown in Table 7.

Table 7: Constraints Mentioned in Trade Facilitation Plans in BIMSTEC Region

Issue/Plan	SASEC Trade Facilitation Framework	SASEC Operational Plan	ASEAN Trade Facilitation Action Plan	BIMSTEC Transport Connectivity Masterplan
Soft Infrastructure	X			
Revised Kyoto Convention	X	X	X	X
WTO Trade Facilitation Agreement			X	X
Rationalization of clearance documents	X	X		X
Customs ICT	X	X	X	X
Automation in other agencies	X	X		
National single window	X	X	X	X
Trade information portals	X	X	X	
E-trading				X
Risk management		X	X	
Authorized economic operators	X	X	X	
Post-clearance auditing		X	X	
Pre-arrival processing	X	X	X	
Advanced rulings		X	X	
Transit systems		X	X	
CCC/NTTFC Committees	X	X	X	
Time-release studies			X	
Customs legislation	X			
Mutual recognition agreements	X	X	X	
Hard Infrastructure				
Land border infrastructure	X	X		X
Inland clearance depots	X	X		X
Land ports	X	X		X
Container freight stations				
Test laboratories		X		
Trade Logistics				
Port community systems		X		
Institutional and Capacity Building	X	X	X	X

BIMSTEC = Bay of Bengal Initiative for Multi-Sectoral Technical and Economic Cooperation, CCC = Customs Coordination Committee, ICT = information and communication technology, NTTFC = national transport and trade facilitation committee, SASEC = South Asia Subregional Economic Cooperation, WTO = World Trade Organization.

Source: Asian Development Bank.

In principle, all these aspects should be included in the Strategic Framework, but having over 20 subcomponents could be unwieldy, leading to a possible loss of focus. It was therefore deemed prudent to consolidate these challenges into components and sub-components, similar to the approach used in the SASEC framework and the BIMSTEC Master Plan for Transport Connectivity. The chosen structure is to have four main components: soft infrastructure, hard infrastructure, trade logistics, and capacity building. These are subdivided into subcomponents, each with its specific series of sub-strategies and sub-goals. The chosen subcomponents are:

Soft Infrastructure

- Increased remote processing and clearance;
- Automation;
- Rationalizing documentation;
- Applying advanced procedures;
- Complying with international agreements and conventions;
- Transit systems;
- Cooperation mechanisms;
- Customs legislation;
- MRAs; and
- Time-release studies.

Hard Infrastructure

- Land border infrastructure;
- ICDs;
- Land ports;
- CFSs; and
- Testing stations and laboratories.

Trade Logistics

- Changes in trade logistics; and
- Linkages between NSWs and PCSs.

Cooperation and Capacity Building

- Regional cooperation;
- Mutual cooperation in capacity-building; and
- Capacity building.

Soft infrastructure has significantly more sub-components than the other three components. This is partly a reflection of its wider scope and partly because advances in this component are considered the most important for achieving the strategic framework's overall goal.

Guiding Principles

It is important to include guiding principles in any strategic plan to clearly understand the basis on which it evolved. In general, these principles also relate to how the strategic framework will be conceptually implemented.

The guiding principles of the SASEC Trade Facilitation Framework include:

- country ownership;
- pragmatism and results orientation;
- flexibility and responsiveness to the needs of member countries;
- cooperation with SASEC's neighboring countries;
- participation of the private sector; and
- partnerships with development partners.

The SASEC Operational Plan does not have guiding principles, but the implementation section indicates the plan should adhere to the following principles:

- country ownership;
- demand-driven, pragmatic, and results-orientated;
- partnerships with stakeholders, including IFIs;
- innovative and have flexible institutional arrangements;
- promotes resource mobilization;
- encourages strong knowledge support; and
- applies greater involvement of the private sector.

The ASEAN Trade Facilitation Framework cites several guiding principles that were later used in the formulation of their Trade Facilitation Action Plan. These were:

- transparency;
- communications and consultation;
- simplification and efficiency;
- non-discrimination;
- consistency and predictability;
- harmonization and mutual recognition;
- modernization and use of new technology;
- due process;
- cooperation; and
- private-sector orientation.

The BIMSTEC Master Plan for Transport Connectivity has a section on principles, but these relate to the specific purpose of the plan rather than giving guidance on the principles behind the plan's development.

The BIMSTEC strategic framework should articulate the principles applied in its advancement. These would likely be similar to those in the SASEC Trade Facilitation Framework, despite the need for clear a separation between SASEC and BIMSTEC. This is because they are logical principles that can be applied to any trade facilitation planning, irrespective of geographical considerations. The chief principles will include:

- country ownership;
- results orientation combined with pragmatism;
- flexibility and responsiveness to country needs;
- reforms and modernization;
- active participation of the private sector;
- partnerships with development partners; and
- mutual cooperation.

Proposed Monitoring Mechanisms

The strategic framework sets out the goals in a defining statement that outlines measurable achievements that fulfill the overall strategy to realize the mission and vision. Each sub-component will also be supported by subsidiary objectives aimed at realizing the overall goal. These sub-goals will need to be carefully monitored to gauge the rate of progress in the implementation of each sub-component. The guiding principles discussed above emphasize the need to be results-orientated. While monitoring will identify the progress made, it can also be effective for promoting motivation and momentum to implement improvements and demonstrate to stakeholders that positive changes are being realized transparently.

Evidence from similar regional initiatives suggests the collection and collation of data required for monitoring can be particularly problematic. The receipt of the necessary information data can be spasmodic and often fails to represent a specific point in time, because data may be submitted at different times. In general, the easier the monitoring mechanism in terms of workload, the more likely it will be that data will be tendered on time. Different monitoring mechanisms should be applied for the four components:

- **Soft infrastructure.** The TFA covers almost all sub-components. The goal is that by 2030 all BIMSTEC countries will have achieved the category goals suggested in section 4.2.2. Countries must submit notifications to the WTO periodically and the WTO assigns an implementation percentage that is publicly available on its website. For Bhutan, comparative data will be needed, either via Bhutan customs or through a BIMSTEC focal person;
- **Hard infrastructure.** The goals of this component consist of physical structures and can be measured by completed construction projects. Both the SASEC Operational Plan and the BIMSTEC Master Plan for Transport Connectivity are predominantly based on individual project monitoring. Suitable hard infrastructure projects should be submitted by member states to the BIMSTEC Secretariat. Information on the progress of these projects could then be submitted by national focal persons annually;
- **Trade logistics.** This component covers the provision of logistics systems, and trade trends that suggest a dual approach would be appropriate. The provision of these systems can be monitored by the national focal person based on the implementation of automated applications and their links. Identifying trade trends probably requires independent external expertise, possibly provided by an IFI. Under the TFA, countries have to undertake time-release studies, which can be an important measuring tool for checking whether processing

times at borders are getting faster or not. It is important that this monitoring is extended to cover the largest BIMSTEC ports and land borders; and

- **Training and capacity-building.** This component includes both internal training for border organizations and training and capacity-building by external agencies, such as the IFIs, the WCO, and the WTO, or by corresponding agencies in other BIMSTEC countries. Only the capacity-building by external agencies should be monitored, and this could be done by national focal persons.

The focal point for information relating to the implementation of the framework in each country could be the National Trade Facilitation Committee or a National Transport and Trade Facilitation Committee because they are also interested in this information and may be repositories for relevant data. Progress information should only be submitted and collated on an annual basis. The sub-component goals should also be reviewed annually by a BIMSTEC trade facilitation working group, and, if necessary, adjusted based on the progress achieved, funding availability, and the emergence of other priority constraints. The working group on the Agreement on Trade Facilitation for the BIMSTEC Free Trade Area could consider taking on this role. BIMSTEC should disseminate annual achievement updates of the goals through its website to ensure the strategic framework remains relevant and continues to be a "live" planning document.

It may be prudent to have a midterm review of the strategic framework in 2025 to take stock of the progress that has been achieved. By this time, the economic impact of the COVID-19 pandemic and other factors should have played out and trade returned to normal levels. For this reason, it is not intended to use trade growth as a goal or target, as has been applied in other strategic plans. This is due to the current pandemic-induced economic downturn, high commodity prices, global inflation levels, and conflicts combining to indicate volatility and the lack of a clear growth pattern in the immediate future. The midterm review will enable, if needed, the realignment of sub-component goals encountered in the course of implementation, over and above any annual adjustment such as the inclusion of additional hard infrastructure projects.

BIMSTEC TRADE FACILITATION STRATEGIC FRAMEWORK 2030

Introduction and Background

BIMSTEC's core functions are promoting free trade and increasing cross-border investment. Trade was identified as one of the six sectors of BIMSTEC cooperation at its inception in 1997 in recognition of the important role trade can play in both national and regional economic growth. Expanding intraregional trade between member states can become the cornerstone of their regional economic cooperation.

BIMSTEC has adopted a twin approach to tackling constraints to regional trade. The BIMSTEC Free Trade Area initiative is specifically planned to help eliminate or minimize tariff barriers affecting intraregional trade, whereas the parallel trade facilitation program is designed to tackle the nontariff barriers affecting overall trade in the region. This strategic framework addresses the latter, providing a structured approach to enhancing regional trade facilitation in the period up to 2030.

Internationally, setting up free trade areas and trade agreements have faced significant headwinds in recent years. The implementation of this strategic framework does not depend on a BIMSTEC Free Trade Area agreement being ratified, although its implementation would be expected to increase intraregional trade. Most nontariff barriers addressed in this strategic framework exist equally concerning both intraregional and external trade, thus the need for a comprehensive approach covering trade in general irrespective of its origin or destination and mode of transport.

Trade facilitation initiatives in the region have so far focused on gradually eliminating nontariff barriers that affect cross-border trading. This initial concentration has mainly been on promoting improvements in land border infrastructure and enhancing customs processing by increasing the use of automated systems. More recently, this approach has broadened to include other main border agencies through the establishment of national single windows. Constraints in trade facilitation are the leading nontariff barriers that have directly resulted in higher costs being incurred by the trading community. Empirical research and estimates on the impact of nontariff barriers suggest that these are far more trade-restrictive than tariffs.

The trade facilitation situation in BIMSTEC countries differs significantly. Various international trade facilitation performance indicators suggest India and Thailand are the most advanced, followed by Bangladesh, Myanmar, and Sri Lanka, with landlocked Bhutan and Nepal the least advanced at this stage. To a certain extent, this coincides with the progress these countries have made in introducing more automated applications, although other factors have also played a part. These differences need to be acknowledged within a common framework approach. Here, proposed strategies apply to all member states to a greater or lesser extent, but with national variations in their importance reflecting their individual situations. Even though trade facilitation has improved considerably across the BIMSTEC region over the past decade, it still remains appreciably below those of most developed countries and the market leaders in adjacent regions.

The impact of the COVID-19 pandemic on the region has been significant. This included a temporary downturn in trade and the need for adjustments in the way clearances are undertaken in some member states, manifested by an increased reliance on automated systems — "process distancing." Although the pandemic will likely continue to affect the implementation of the strategic framework in the short- to medium-term, it also represents an opportunity to embrace new approaches and technologies designed to enhance performance in an evolving trade facilitation situation.

Framework Scope and Structural Logic

Framework Scope

The traditional definitions of trade facilitation have tended to focus on the simplification of border processing and procedures and the physical locations where these are conducted. Because of this, trade facilitation in the BIMSTEC region has mainly concentrated on enhancing border infrastructure, increasing the automation of customs processing, and setting up national trade facilitation bodies. In recent years, the scope of these initiatives has gradually broadened to encompass additional border agencies and the advancement of supporting infrastructure located away from the borders. This wider scope reflects a gradual change of emphasis from the specific needs of border authorities to being more oriented to the demands of the trading community and the need to drive down cross-border trading costs.

This process is set to continue throughout the strategic framework timeframe with even further broadening of its scope reflecting the changes in trade practices and logistics relating to the movement of international trade. Because border clearances are merely a link in an international logistics chain, a more holistic approach is required, whereby trade facilitation concentrates increasingly on the time, cost, and reliability of processing trade movements on behalf of stakeholders. Performance improvements can be achieved through a combination of streamlining documentation, even greater use of automated systems, more modern infrastructure at borders and inland, and enhanced cooperation among stakeholders.

Framework Structure

Figure 6 shows the logic applied to the development of the strategic framework.

Visions

BIMSTEC's overall objectives are to promote technological and economic cooperation among its South Asian and Southeast Asian member states. The joint declaration of the 4th BIMSTEC Summit in Kathmandu in August 2018 resolved to consolidate and deepen cooperation among member states to make BIMSTEC an effective platform for promoting peace, prosperity, and sustainability. The overarching BIMSTEC vision for this framework reflects this resolution for a *"peaceful, prosperous and sustainable BIMSTEC region."*

Figure 6: Framework Logic

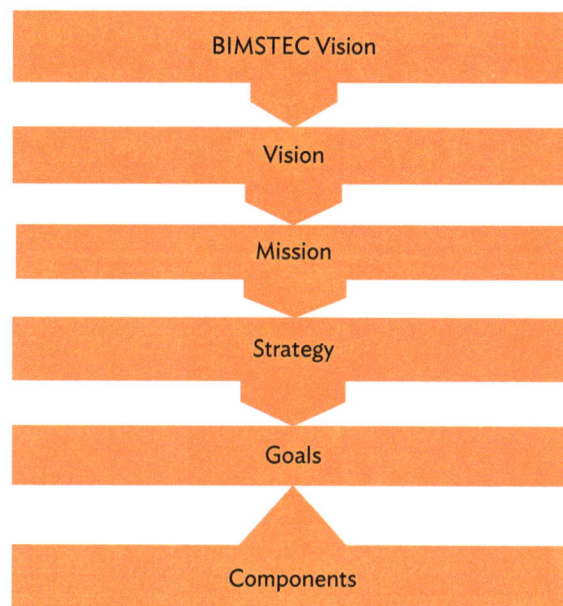

BIMSTEC Vision

Vision

Mission

Strategy

Goals

Components

BIMSTEC Bay of Bengal Initiative for Multi-Sectoral Technical and Economic Cooperation
Source: Asian Development Bank. 2014. *South Asia Subregional Economic Cooperation Trade Facilitation Strategic Framework 2014-2018*. Manila.

The strategic framework's specific vision should be compliant with this overarching vision, but be more focused on the evolving trade facilitation conditions and the changing demands of stakeholders. The framework's vision is the *"promotion of BIMSTEC trade through the more efficient movement of international freight passing through its land, sea and air borders."*

Mission

The mission statement describes the overall purpose of the strategic framework to realize this vision. The framework's mission is to *"facilitate the more efficient movement of compliant trade through BIMSTEC borders by the application of advanced clearance practices, combined with supporting investment in 'hard' and 'soft' infrastructure."*

Strategy

The strategy statement articulates the approach to fulfilling the mission. The strategic framework's strategy is the *"more widespread implementation of advanced international best practices in cargo clearance processing, complemented by investment in border and inland clearance facilities."*

Goals

The strategy goals indicate the intended results of implementing the strategy and define how its achievement can be measured. The strategic framework's goals are *"compliance with international trade facilitation agreements and best practices incorporating increased levels of automation, expansion of infrastructure supporting expedited border transit times, and promotion of enhanced cooperation and coordination between member states."*

Components

The components identify the different areas of trade facilitation to be addressed by the strategic framework and how they will be implemented to realize the overall goal. The four components focus on advancing 'soft' and 'hard' infrastructure, trade logistics, and capacity-building.

Compliance with Trade Facilitation Agreements in the BIMSTEC Region

BIMSTEC countries are all members of other regional cooperation initiatives. These include ASEAN and SAARC, as well as the ADB's South Asian Economic Cooperation and Greater Mekong Subregion initiatives, all of which have trade facilitation programs. It is imperative the strategic framework is both compliant with and complements these agreements to which member states are signatories. In many cases, they have adopted a two-stage approach based on initially establishing a strategic framework that is then followed by an action plan identifying how the framework will be implemented. This strategic framework differs because it adopts a combined approach to cover both stages within a single document. This methodology is designed to speed up the implementation of the proposed strategies once the strategic framework has been endorsed by member states.

Trade Facilitation Constraints

BIMSTEC's trade facilitation situation has improved significantly over the last decade with all member states now having some form of customs automation and upgraded infrastructure at primary land borders and commencing the planning or implementation of national single windows linking all the main border agencies. At the same time, the changing external trading situation has been putting increased or new stakeholder demands on border agencies. Because of this, an inevitable lag has occurred in being able to meet these demands and the supply-side responses by the border agencies.

The strategic framework is designed to close this gap in a structured manner. Box 1 shows some of the constraints the framework seeks to address. The relatively large number of constraints reflects the significant differences in the trade facilitation environment between member states, and it is acknowledged that not all these problems are necessarily present in each country.

Box 1: Trade Facilitation Constraints

Soft Infrastructure

- **Direct interface between border authorities and brokers.** Current methodologies still require high levels of face-to-face contact between customs and traders' representatives when lodging hard copy documentation and during inspection and examination routines;
- **Levels of automation.** Despite increased investment in automated systems, some member states' border authorities continue to rely on manual processing and signatures, using the system for transaction recording rather than automated processing. Developing the national single windows remains problematic due to the lower levels of automation of some of the other border agencies, as well as institutional difficulties in integrating all parties into this communal application;
- **Rationalization of clearance documentation.** The main documentation required for import and export clearance has been reduced but not to the levels present in developed countries, and reliance on original documents, manual signatures, and high numbers of required copies remain high, despite automation;
- **Limited use of risk management and approved economic operators.** Overall examination and inspection levels remain high in member states despite the widespread introduction of risk management and channeling techniques. The numbers of approved economic operators and risk management-supporting post-clearance audits are low;
- **Lack of pre-arrival processing and application of advanced rulings.** Border authorities continue to rely on commencing shipment processing after the goods physically arrive at the border rather than starting the process in advance if the documentation is available. Applying advanced rulings to eliminate classification and valuation disputes is still limited when clearing imports;
- **Compliance with international trade facilitation agreements.** Member states are at different stages in the ratification and implementation of the World Trade Organization's Trade Facilitation Agreement and the World Customs Organization's Revised Kyoto Convention and Standards to Secure and Facilitate Trade Framework, which are all aimed at adopting international best practices;
- **Limited use of inland transit systems.** Most cargoes continue to be cleared at points of entry, rather than close to the points of final delivery, due to expensive transit control systems and the incidence of almost "double clearance" requirements;
- **Poor institutional cooperation.** Border agencies often work in isolation relative to their individual responsibilities rather than being part of a cohesive clearance team. Cooperation and coordination can also be limited between authorities on either side of the borders or between their relevant ministries in adjacent countries;
- **Reliance on outdated customs legislation.** Because trade facilitation needs to respond to changes in the external trade environment, dated customs legislation can inhibit the application of automated processing and the introduction of advanced processing techniques;
- **Lack of mutual recognition agreements.** Certain imported products, such as foodstuffs and electrical products, often require tests to be undertaken post-arrival due to the absence of mutual recognition agreements with authorities in the exporting country; and
- **Limited use of performance monitoring.** The low use or absence of monitoring tools, such as time-release studies, make it difficult for stakeholders to measure whether or not performance improvements are being made from changes in processing, investment, and capacity building.

continued on next page

Box continued

Hard Infrastructure

- **Need for additional border facilities.** Despite significant investments since 2000 on land border infrastructure, this has not always been reflected in enhanced transit times; this is sometimes due to poor ergonomics and other associated design aspects. Many secondary borders remain congested as they await funding for their modernization;
- **Demand for more inland clearance depots.** Most imports clear at points of entry, rather than near final destinations, due to the lack of approved clearance facilities in inland areas of concentrated import/export demand. This results in additional transport costs and time. The shortage of inland clearance depots also risks increasing dwell times and congestion at the larger BIMSTEC seaports;
- **Expansion of land ports.** Land port construction adjacent to borders often merely moves the point of congestion from border control zones to a few kilometers inland without necessarily expediting transit times. Some countries also levy a charge to use land ports without providing any added-value services;
- **Shortage of container freight stations.** There are often not enough container freight stations outside port areas to be able to efficiently handle less-than-containerload cargoes, resulting in the delayed clearance of consolidation traffic and congestion at port terminals; and
- **Insufficient numbers of test laboratories.** Products arriving at land and sea borders requiring test certificates often require samples to be sent to distant inland laboratories for testing, resulting in clearance delays. For perishable products, these delays can sometimes result in the total loss of the shipment.

Trade Logistics

- **Global value chain risks.** Clearance delays at borders can invalidate the benefits of member states in attracting global value chain traffic due to the inherent supply risks to production line manufacturing;
- **Adaptability of trade facilitation to advanced logistical concepts.** The latest logistical practices employed by stakeholders, such as vendor-managed inventory, e-commerce, and new trading terms, are not always compatible with traditional clearance processing methodologies; and
- **Constraints in linking national single windows to port community systems.** Where these exist, there is often no online interface between the two systems. This compromises the tracking and tracing capability of port community systems because of the lack of data on the clearance status of shipments.

Institutional and Capacity-Building

- **Duplicated processing with automated and manual systems operating in parallel.** The main reason for this is that border agency officers have not fully bought into the system. This lack of trust means that they revert to manual processing using the system as a transaction-recording application rather than as a processing tool;
- **Insufficient skills upgrading.** Changes in trade facilitation require new skills and raising the overall levels of professionalism, but border authorities often have limited training programs and can suffer skills losses from high staff turnover and rotation regimes;
- **Shortage of experienced information technology personnel.** Border agencies have problems in attracting and retaining quality personnel to maintain and advance increasingly sophisticated information technology applications due to government pay scale constraints. Information technology staff turnover is a particular problem due to intense competition from the private sector; and
- **Limited cooperation between authorities in member states.** The trade facilitation environment varies significantly between member states. The most economically advanced countries have not established a mechanism to assist the least advanced ones, which continue to rely mainly on external programs provided or funded by international funding institutions.

Source: Asian Development Bank.

BIMSTEC Trade Facilitation Strategic Framework 2030

Framework Overview

Figure 7 shows the strategic framework diagrammatically using the logic in Figure 6. The visions, mission, and overall strategy combine to define the reasons for the strategic framework, culminating in the definitions of its intended goals. The framework's core constituent is achieving the overall goal by progressing the proposals contained in each of the components to address the constraints highlighted in Box 1. Each component identifies specific problems concerning that component, followed by a strategy indicating pathways toward its resolution. These subgoals can be used to monitor progress being realized in the implementation of the framework.

Figure 7: Reasoning behind the BIMSTEC Trade Facilitation Strategic Framework 2030

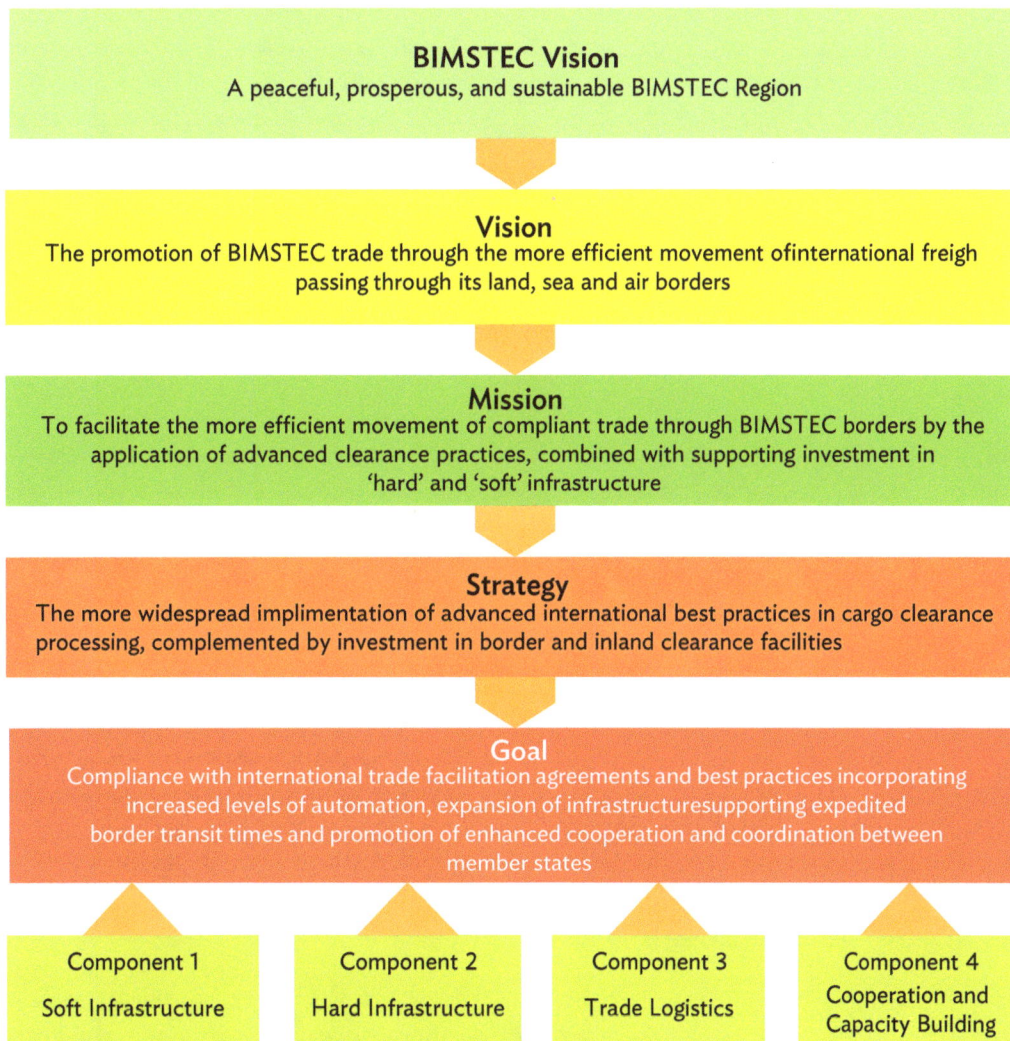

BIMSTEC Vision
A peaceful, prosperous, and sustainable BIMSTEC Region

Vision
The promotion of BIMSTEC trade through the more efficient movement ofinternational freigh passing through its land, sea and air borders

Mission
To facilitate the more efficient movement of compliant trade through BIMSTEC borders by the application of advanced clearance practices, combined with supporting investment in 'hard' and 'soft' infrastructure

Strategy
The more widespread implimentation of advanced international best practices in cargo clearance processing, complemented by investment in border and inland clearance facilities

Goal
Compliance with international trade facilitation agreements and best practices incorporating increased levels of automation, expansion of infrastructuresupporting expedited border transit times and promotion of enhanced cooperation and coordination between member states

Component 1 Soft Infrastructure

Component 2 Hard Infrastructure

Component 3 Trade Logistics

Component 4 Cooperation and Capacity Building

BIMSTEC Bay of Bengal Initiative for Multi-Sectoral Technical and Economic Cooperation
Source: Asian Development Bank.

Priorities have not generally been included in the framework because member states are at differing levels of advancement in their trade facilitation situations. However, a common priority is to reduce the time and cost of border transactions, be they at land borders, seaports, airports, or inland clearance depots. Enhancing the performance of border agencies will only be possible through procedural changes, supported by further investment in 'soft' infrastructure. Investments in 'hard' infrastructure at borders and clearance facilities can often fail to generate the anticipated facilitation benefits unless reinforced by parallel improvements in the processing performance of these facilities.

Component 1: Soft Infrastructure

Increased Remote Processing and Clearances

Constraint

Modern border processing is designed around the concept of minimizing the interface between customs and other border agencies and the wider trading community, thereby promoting 'process distancing'. Yet, clearance activities continue to rely heavily on face-to-face contact between border authorities and traders or their agents. Advanced processing methodologies call for clearances to be predominantly online, with limited direct interfacing between the parties except for when shipments require inspection and examination or that are in dispute.

Strategy

BIMSTEC will encourage member states to progressively increase the use of online processing and e-clearances, particularly at land, maritime, and aviation borders, and at inland clearance depots.

Goal

Most import and export clearances in the member states should be processed by automated systems, and confirmation of their clearance and release posted online to traders or their agents, thereby limiting the need for face-to-face contact.

Automation

Constraint

All BIMSTEC customs have computer-based systems for collecting and processing data. In some countries, these systems are predominantly used to record transactions rather than for automated processing of declarations. Manual and automated processing is sometimes used in parallel, thereby increasing the processing workload and extending clearance times. A challenge has been getting personnel to buy into or trust the systems as a processing tool. Automation can sometimes be perceived as a threat to job security, rather than making tasks easier, and as potentially eroding the discretionary powers of border officials.

Customs authorities have invested heavily in automated processing systems, but this is not necessarily the case with some of the other border agencies, such as quarantine, veterinary, and trading standards. The clearance processes by these authorities often tend to be the primary cause of long delays on specific cargo at borders. The planning and establishment of national single windows are bringing investments in automated systems at these agencies to the fore to enable them to link into the window.

National single windows allow traders and their agents to lodge standardized information just once at a single electronic data entry point to fulfill all import, export, and transit-related regulatory requirements. This data required by border agencies is then available online in this consolidated database so that each border authority can clear shipments electronically and customs can authorize final release after verifying that all other parties have approved the clearance. Most BIMSTEC countries have either committed to establishing national single windows or are in the process of doing so, but their slow implementation reflects the challenges in setting up these complex systems and maximizing their institutional coverage.

Trade facilitation is generally about compliance and traders have identified difficulties in accessing comprehensive information on the requirements needed to be compliant. Most member states have addressed this situation by establishing trade information portals, but the information provided varies significantly between countries.

Strategy

BIMSTEC will encourage all border agencies in member states to maximize the submission and processing of import, export, and transit declarations using automated systems and the clearance of shipments whenever possible without the need for regular manual intervention, other than in the case of shipments requiring inspection or examination.

BIMSTEC will encourage all the other main border agencies to invest in the application of automated processing systems and member states to continue planning, developing, and expanding national single windows and trade information portals.

Goals

Automated processing should become the norm from the e-filing of declarations through to the payment of duties and final release, thereby minimizing manual interventions. All member states should have fully operational national single windows linking all the main border agencies by 2030 and comprehensive trade information portals by 2025.

Rationalization of Documentation

Constraint

There is a relationship between the number of documents required to complete an average import or export transaction and overall clearance times. Studies in the region suggest dwell times for container traffic are often dictated by the time taken for importers or their customs agents to collect the various hard copy documents to enable a declaration to be lodged with customs, rather than the actual physical customs processing times. Despite some progress in reducing the documentary requirements for clearances in member states, they generally still exceed those of countries with more advanced trade facilitation environments. In some BIMSTEC countries, increased documentary requirements are required for certain export products, thus potentially compromising the aims of national export promotion schemes.

Customs agents continue to complain about the large number of copies of documents needed for clearance. Because all customs authorities have automated systems containing this information, the need for so many supporting hard copies appears questionable. Another issue is the need to produce original documentation specifically at the time of lodging. This requirement becomes particularly difficult if the documentation needs to be authorized or stamped by an external party, such as a bank. In most developed countries, all clearance documentation is submitted in e-form with electronic signatures where required and with originals only being submitted later in exchange for the clearance receipt.

Harmonization of the documentation required for a clearance is still lacking, despite recommendations by the Simplification and Harmonization of Trade Procedures (SITPRO) and the World Customs Organization. While automation has tended to standardize the layouts of customs declaration forms, there has been little or no standardization of other documents, for example, sanitary, phytosanitary, veterinary, and standards requirements. Each BIMSTEC country tends to have its own formats and often does not recognize the validity of the documentation from other member states.

Strategy

BIMSTEC will encourage member states to reduce the number of original documents and copies required to support import, export, or transit declarations. Clearance should increasingly become based on e-submissions rather than relying on the submission of original documents at the time of e-filing. BIMSTEC will also encourage the use of international format documentation wherever possible.

Goals

A reduction in documentary requirements by customs to less than six core import or export documents to enable a clearance by 2025 (excluding those required by other border agencies). Submission of original documentation should not be mandatory at the time of e-filing and the number of copy documents should be reduced to less than five supporting copies by 2030.

Application of Advanced Procedures

Constraint

Risk management recognizes that as trade expands it will not be physically possible to examine every shipment without causing congestion and delays at seaports and borders. It also appreciates that most shipments are likely to be compliant, especially those involving regular traders. Risk management is designed to facilitate the movement of cargoes belonging to compliant traders by identifying which shipments present a risk and need to be examined and which can be cleared based solely on documentary controls. Most automated customs control systems have risk assessment applications in their software. While the concept of risk assessment is generally accepted by all BIMSTEC customs authorities, high levels of examination persist in many countries for various reasons, and the application of risk management by other border agencies is often limited.

Authorized economic operator programs are an extension of the risk management concept. The logic behind this is that large regular traders, such as multinational corporations and large corporations, represent a low non-compliance risk, and this should be reflected in higher service levels and enhanced facilitation. Although some member states have authorized economic operator programs, the number of approved traders remains relatively small, and others have yet to fully embrace the program despite their acceptance of the concept.

An important support mechanism to the authorized economic operator or 'trusted trader' initiatives is post-clearance auditing. Under this concept, imported goods are automatically green channeled, thereby enabling their rapid clearance from seaports or borders but on the condition that customs can later undertake a physical examination of the documentation and/or the shipment post-clearance if deemed necessary. All BIMSTEC countries either have post-clearance operations or are training officers in post-clearance auditing techniques, but its application so far has been limited.

Various other advanced techniques designed to expedite clearances exist, including pre-arrival processing, whereby importers or exporters submit declarations and documentation in advance of the physical arrival of their shipments. Here, the process starts earlier and consequently should result in faster clearance on arrival. Another common application is advanced rulings, whereby exporters or importers submit details of their shipments being traded and obtain an advanced ruling that classifies their product under the harmonized system coding and hence likely duties depending on the country of origin or value. This helps eliminate disputes at borders during the later assessment and examination procedures. Neither of these techniques is yet widely practiced in the region.

Strategy

BIMSTEC will encourage member states to reduce overall physical inspection and examination levels through the widespread application of risk management and the approval of more authorized economic operators or "trusted traders". This will expedite border clearance, even though it may require increased post-clearance auditing to ensure compliance.

BIMSTEC will encourage member states to introduce pre-arrival processing, provided that the necessary supporting data is available in advance, and that advanced-ruling services should become more widely accessible.

Goals

By applying risk management and expanding authorized economic operator programs, the percentage of green channel shipments should gradually increase and physical examination levels decrease, compared to 2020 levels. Post-audit capabilities should be expanded by training more specialist units, pre-arrival processing should be permitted in all member states by 2025, and advanced ruling capacities expanded to meet potential future demand.

Compliance with International Agreements and Conventions

Constraint

BIMSTEC countries have ratified several international agreements and conventions. The main one is the WTO's Trade Facilitation Agreement (TFA) which is a benchmark for modern trade facilitation practices. All BIMSTEC countries, except Bhutan, are signatories and are at differing implementation stages. That Bhutan is not a WTO member should not inhibit its adoption of the agreement's recommendations. Two other important agreements are the Revised Kyoto Convention and the SAFE Framework.

Progress in implementing the TFA can be used to gauge the progress being made in trade facilitation in individual countries. The enactment of the articles in the agreement by the WTO's developing member countries is categorized as A, B, and C, with A being full implementation, B part implementation, and C signifying that implementation will need external assistance. The agreement has flexibility as not all the technical measures are mandatory, with some only requiring best efforts. It allows each developing country member to determine when it will implement a measure and determine whether external support is needed.

Strategy

BIMSTEC will encourage member states to implement the articles and recommendations contained in the Trade Facilitation Agreement, the Revised Kyoto Convention, and the SAFE Framework, irrespective of whether they have been ratified by the member states or not.

Goals

India, Thailand	TFA: all Category B/C to A by the end of 2024;
Bangladesh, Sri Lanka	TFA: all Category C to A or B by the end of 2023 and all Category B to A by the end of 2026
Myanmar, Nepal, Bhutan	TFA: 20% Category A, 40% Category B, and 40% Category C by the end of 2023, 40% Category A and 40% Category B and only 20% Category C by the end of 2026

Transit Systems

Constraint

The modern trend in the clearance of imports is to transfer the main procedures from points of entry to inland locations, such as inland clearance depots or bonded warehouses, closer to the importers or end-users. This approach facilitates trade as the main clearance processing takes place closer to the concentrations of demand, making it easier for importers or their agents to lodge entry documentation. More importantly, this greatly reduces the risk of congestion at border points of entry because cargoes can be moved faster to these inland facilities through the land borders or seaports.

The standard transit system used in developed countries is that the inland movement travels under bond. This well-established system is dependent on three elements: trust, finance, and security—importers or their agents are reputable so the cargo is considered less likely to "disappear," the importers or their agents have sufficient funds to lodge bond payments, and movements between borders or ports to inland locations are carried sealed units. A residual problem is the transit of import cargoes by road where there are constraints in the road network and/or concerns over the security of road transport. For land borders, the transit from a border is often in vehicles that cannot be easily sealed. For containerized traffic by road to landlocked member states, a tracking system has already been trialed using electronic seals, thus eliminating the need for bonding routines.

Strategy

BIMSTEC will encourage member states to adopt the more widespread application of transit procedures, thereby reducing the proportion of imports needing to be fully clearance at the point of entry and to promote the faster movement of transit traffic destined to or from the landlocked member states.

Goals

Growth in the percentage of container shipments clearing at inland clearance depots or off-dock container freight stations, resulting in lower dwell times at seaport terminals and land borders and reduced transit times for containers traveling between seaports and the landlocked member states.

Cooperation Mechanisms

Constraint

Institutional customs cooperation is three-dimensional. The first dimension is cooperation with the trading community, the second is between other customs authorities, and the third is between customs and the other border agencies. Firstly, all BIMSTEC countries have established National Trade Facilitation Committees or equivalents, although their spheres of influence may vary, as well as their degree of private sector participation. Secondly, cooperation through regional cooperation mechanisms. BIMSTEC has its Customs Working Group working to finalize aspects of the Free Trade Area Agreement, and this could become a customs cooperation committee, similar to those in other regional initiatives covering member states.

The third dimension is cooperation between the various agencies at borders. This is critical in achieving optimal performance, as clearances are often a "team" undertaking with each player participating in a coordinated manner. At land borders, the TFA encourages officials on either side of the border to meet regularly to discuss coordination aspects, such as agreements on working days and hours and queueing strategies between border posts when congestion is present.

Strategy

BIMSTEC will encourage national trade facilitation committees in their efforts to plan and promote improvements in trade facilitation performance, together with the active participation of border agencies and the private sector. BIMSTEC will consider the formation of a customs coordination committee should there be demand from member states. BIMSTEC will also encourage regular exchanges between clearance authorities at borders and with their partner land border posts.

Goals

National trade facilitation committees should include representatives from the private sector to address the broadening scope of trade facilitation with changes in trading methods and practices. BIMSTEC will establish a BIMSTEC customs coordination committee if requested by the member states.

Customs Legislation

Constraint

Countries have varying forms of legislation covering trade facilitation. For customs services, the general approach is a customs act setting out the roles and responsibilities of customs services, followed by subsidiary rules and regulations determining how the act is implemented operationally. Acts can only usually be amended by parliament, whereas rules and regulations can be changed by ministries or by customs themselves. In general, this secondary legislation (rules and regulations) is regularly adjusted to reflect changes in practices and procedures. In some cases, secondary legislation is included in an act, making it more comprehensive in scope, but making changes becomes more difficult to implement at short notice.

Trade facilitation is taking place in a dynamic market environment requiring regular changes in practices and procedures and the adoption of advanced customs approaches with the increased use of automation. In general, these changes can be made by issuing new rules or regulations. A problem arises when these advanced procedures cannot be implemented because of a customs act. In many BIMSTEC countries, the core customs legislation is becoming increasingly dated and this legislation needs to be updated when it impedes the introduction of advanced practices and increased automation.

Strategy

BIMSTEC will encourage the modernization of customs legislation, either in the form of new or revised customs acts or supporting rules and regulations to facilitate planned changes in customs practices and procedures designed to enhance performance.

Goals

Customs acts should be reviewed every 10 years and updated if they are not compliant with international agreements and best practices—unless this can be dealt with by regulations not requiring specific parliamentary endorsement.

Mutual Recognition Agreements

Constraint

There are only a few mutual recognition agreements between the BIMSTEC countries because the validity of tests and standards done in one country is often not accepted by another. This means traders in the importing countries have to have tests conducted by their national bodies to obtain national certification, even if testing has already been conducted in the exporting county. In some countries, testing is required on every individual shipment, as opposed to type-approval certification. An additional constraint is that many of these testing centers in the region do not meet international approval standards.

The absence of mutual recognition agreements and the need for constant retesting is a significant nontariff barrier in the BIMSTEC region, especially for food and electrical products. If more mutual recognition agreements were negotiated, it would enable the establishment of protocols whereby authorities in an importing country could access certificates online from the export country to either clear the goods in the absence of the necessary national certificate or check the validity of documents being produced by importers. This would also apply to certificates of origin, as well as sanitary, phytosanitary, and trading standards certificates.

Strategy

BIMSTEC will encourage member states to increase the number of mutual recognition agreements between them, particularly for regular import and export products requiring certification.

Goals

A 50% increase in mutual recognition agreements between member states by 2025 and 100% by 2030, using 2020 as the base year.

Time-Release Studies

Constraint

The WCO's time-release studies are a tool to measure trade facilitation performance with a view to improvements. Data is collected on the time taken for cargoes to proceed through each clearance process from the time of arrival of the mode of transport until the time goods exit the airports, seaports, or road borders. This is sometimes referred to as the border/seaport/airport dwell time. These studies measure the performance of customs activities as they directly relate to trade facilitation at borders, thus allowing interventions to be developed to further improve performance.

Time-release studies can be an important benchmarking mechanism to help identify progress in the strategic framework's implementation. They have been conducted in all BIMSTEC countries, but with particular emphasis on land borders. The WCO's model may need to be extended to undertake these studies at seaports due to the increased number of parties being involved.

Strategy

BIMSTEC will encourage member states to undertake time-release studies at their most important borders on a scheduled basis.

Goals

Establishment of effective monitoring systems on improvements in clearance performance in member states based on the results of time-release studies.

Component 2: Hard Infrastructure

Resolving soft infrastructure constraints is critical for enhancing trade facilitation, but this needs to be supported by investments in complementary hard infrastructure. The extent of this infrastructure can have a direct impact on the efficiency of the borders and the inland clearance of import and export trade. Upgrading infrastructure in regional initiatives, such as under ADB and World Bank programs, have been predominantly project-based.

Land Border Infrastructure

Constraint

Border crossings are breaks in the international logistics chain. The modern trend is for facilities at the land borders to merely serve as checkpoints for freight traffic rather than as final clearance points. This can be done for imports by simple document checks at borders, followed by a visual inspection of vehicles and cargoes, and then allowing shipments to proceed inland to an adjacent land port or inland clearance depot for full clearance processing, thus minimizing border dwell times and congestion.

This approach has been difficult to implement in the BIMSTEC region and in many other developing countries for a variety of reasons. This is in part due to the lack of through-transport, traditional practices and procedures, and the large numbers of small traders. Most border posts continue to act as a final clearance facility with high levels of examinations, thus requiring a more substantial border complex. Every BIMSTEC country either has or is in the process of modernizing its infrastructure at its primary land borders (except Sri Lanka, which has no land borders).

The design of these new border facilities generally complies with international best practices, although in some cases there are concerns that they may be too large, with designs being based on accommodating the delays incurred when using previous processing regimes. The danger exists that these facilities merely move queuing from adjacent border roads into the border control zones without any significant performance improvements to justify the investment. Some designs are not based on "form-follows-function" concepts but on standard designs, whereby the functions have to be fitted into the layout rather than vice versa. Borders have varied profiles and applying standard designs can result in overinvestment with large sprawling layouts with manning constraints, especially when the borders are located in rural environments.

As trade increases, the demand for border processing tends to become progressively devolved, as the origins and destinations of trade expand beyond the primary population centers. Stakeholders want more secondary borders to be upgraded or expanded rather than having to incur additional transport costs traveling farther to use primary border crossings. The need for further investment in smaller border facilities remains an ongoing challenge.

Strategy

BIMSTEC will encourage the prioritization of the construction of border infrastructure at main and secondary land border crossings, based on their processing functionality, projected staffing levels, and future traffic demand.

Goals

Modernization of all BIMSTEC primary land border posts completed by 2025 and main supporting secondary border posts by the latest 2030.

Inland Clearance Depots

Constraint

The concept of land border checkpoints followed by final clearance "inland" may be difficult to realize in the near term due to transit risks, but this is not the case with container traffic. Containers with imports can be sealed at ports and then transported to inland clearance depots closer to the importer or end-user. Doing this not only makes the clearance process easier but also enables inbound containers to move faster through seaports, rather than congesting container terminals while awaiting clearance.

As trade expands, pressure will increase at the main BIMSTEC seaports to raise the percentage of containers being cleared outside port areas. An inland clearance depot's primary role is being an extension of a container yard away from the port and closer to the main points of import and, in some cases export, demand. Dwell times in many BIMSTEC seaports remain high by international comparison, and the need to move more containers rapidly through the ports is growing as a sustainable method for reducing congestion at the maritime interface.

Some countries, including India, already have a national network of inland clearance depots, many of which are rail-connected. Thailand has the region's largest depot and is planning further inland clearance depots. Bangladesh has a facility in Dhaka that is at capacity and requires an additional support facility. Nepal and Bhutan each have inland clearance depots near their borders. Myanmar nominally has these depots in Yangon and plans new depots further inland including at Mandalay. These advances confirm that member states recognize the importance of inland clearance depots and the need for their further development.

Strategy

BIMSTEC will encourage the further construction of inland clearance depots in member states by promoting their inclusion in national development plans and in discussions with relevant authorities and development partners.

Goals

An increase in the number of customs-approved inland clearance depots in all BIMSTEC countries during the period of the strategic framework.

Land Ports

Constraint

The lack of through-transport arrangements and secure inland transport transit regimes for non-containerized cargoes means that most cargo entering through the land borders is cleared at the border. Consequently, additional border clearance infrastructure will need to be built either within border control zones or in their immediate vicinity to accommodate this processing. To reduce congestion at the physical borders, land or dry ports provide a supporting role to the land borders, similar to the role of inland clearance depots in supporting seaport terminals. Land ports are located close to border posts, thus eliminating the need for transit regimes between these facilities and border checkpoints.

Their main function is to clear import and export freight moving by road through adjacent border posts and to accommodate transshipment services where through-transport is not permitted. In some cases, these facilities are located within extended border control zones; in others, they may be several kilometers inland. The construction of supporting land ports can alleviate the need for large infrastructure complexes at the physical borders. An issue for stakeholders is that transferring clearance from the border control zones does not increase costs to traders unless added-value services are provided, such as transshipment and warehousing.

Bangladesh already has a comprehensive network of land ports supporting its borders, Nepal has four land ports, Bhutan one, and Myanmar nominally two. India has adopted the concept of integrated checkpoints, whereby the border checkpoint and land port functions are integrated at a facility in an extended border zone, an integrated check post, as is also the case at the Thai-Myanmar border.

Strategy

BIMSTEC will encourage the construction of land ports designed to relieve congestion at border checkpoints and the provision of added-value services at these facilities if fees are levied.

Goals

All the primary BIMSTEC land borders should be supported by adjacent land ports or integrated checkpoints by 2030, thereby reducing traffic queueing at the physical borders.

Container Freight Stations

Constraint

Container Freight Stations were originally established inside ports to handle less-than-containerload traffic, often using the excess port labor resulting from the transition from conventional general cargo handling to container handling. This role has extended to stuffing and de-stuffing full container load traffic where inland transportation in containerized form is not possible due to road, bridge, or customer access restrictions. These facilities have gradually moved outside the seaports as terminal yards have become more congested and ports now have less excess labor. In effect, container freight stations have a similar role to land ports by supporting maritime borders in handling the clearance of containers at an adjacent location. Border authorities are located at container freight stations in the same way that they are at inland clearance depots and land ports.

The trend in many developed countries has been to gradually phase out on-dock container freight stations to reduce the extent of in-port processing and warehousing, thereby freeing up additional space for container handling and storage. Because BIMSTEC seaports will likely face the same pressures, promoting off-dock container freight stations will become increasingly important. Evidence suggests a significant increase in less-than-containerload shipments will emanate from changing trading practices, such as e-commerce and just-in-time shipping.

Strategy

BIMSTEC will encourage the further opening of off-dock container freight stations to help reduce congestion within BIMSTEC seaport terminals.

Goals

All large BIMSTEC seaports should be supported by licensed off-dock container freight stations by 2025 capable of handling both less-than-containerload and full containerload traffic.

Testing Stations and Laboratories

Constraint

All border agencies should have facilities for the testing of products being traded through their borders. This is to validate the products declared, ensure they meet the standards in the recipient country, and identify illicit goods or false documentation. Customs at most borders have rudimentary testing equipment and mini-laboratories on-site to check for illicit materials, although they often lack the technical expertise and chemicals to undertake more complex testing. Few of the other border agencies, such as sanitary, phytosanitary, and trading standards, have facilities at borders and rely on sending samples off for testing to central laboratories. Most BIMSTEC land borders are far from cities and this procedure can result in significant wait times for getting back test results. Surveys show the chief cause of long delays in clearances at borders is often caused by such testing delays.

There are several challenges relating to the testing of imported products. The first is the approval of agencies in, say, country A to undertake testing and certification on behalf of country B. A significant constraint is that the laboratories in some BIMSTEC countries do not meet international approval standards and therefore the potential for agreeing on mutual recognition agreements is limited. The second is the lack of laboratories close to land borders, including the main ones. This results in delays while products sent from a border to city laboratories are tested and certified, and the results are sent back to the border. If it is not possible to provide more laboratories due to resource limitations (technical, financial, staffing), it will be important to develop online certification methodologies so that test certificates can be issued online at borders immediately after testing to enable the faster release of shipments.

Strategy

BIMSTEC will encourage expanding the capabilities of testing regimes by increasing the number of laboratories in each BIMSTEC country and\or growing the capacities of existing facilities and improving their connectivity to border posts to expedite clearances.

Goals

The numbers and capacities of testing laboratories should be increased during the strategic framework period, and online links established between laboratories and border posts by 2025.

Component 3: Trade Logistics

The use of advanced logistics in most BIMSTEC countries lags behind their use internationally. This is cited as a likely cause of the relatively poor performance of most BIMSTEC countries in the World Bank's Logistics Performance Index. Because external pressures are expected to change the way international trade is conducted, it is vital that trade facilitation in the region can respond to these variations to avoid the possible creation of new nontariff barriers.

Changes in Trade Logistics

Constraint

Global value chains exist in BIMSTEC countries to a greater or lesser extent. These involve the international dispersion of design, production, assembly, marketing, and distribution of services and products. Locating links within these chains is determined by many factors, including technical expertise, wage levels, taxation, capital costs, transport charges, access and reliability, and the ease of moving products internationally to and from the different processes within a chain. Efficient trade facilitation is critical to the viability of these activities. The COVID-19 pandemic has caused firms to reevaluate their global value chains. This may result in reducing reliance on countries within a particular chain or concentrating operations in fewer countries to make the chain more efficient by minimizing the trade facilitation risks involved in the multi-country transfer of components. BIMSTEC countries are well placed to attract more global value chain business, especially from East Asia, but they will need to have attractive trade facilitation environments to ensure that products move rapidly and reliably through their borders and seaports.

The main drivers of advanced logistical applications are to decrease trade costs, enable the faster movement of goods between shippers and consignees, and increase reliability (movements take place as planned to ensure certainty in delivery). Supply chain management of the flow of goods and services involving the movement and storage of raw materials, work-in-process inventories, and finished goods from the point of origin to the point of consumption will become more common in BIMSTEC and other developing country regions. This will require new systems with track and trace capabilities and shipment transparency such that the supply chain becomes less opaque and that any delays at borders and seaports can be flagged.

Strategy

BIMSTEC will encourage member states to respond positively to the use of advanced logistical systems designed to help reduce supply chain costs and transit times without compromising compliance levels.

Goal

Developing and adapting trade facilitation practices to be able to handle advanced trading applications; this should be achieved through enhanced awareness by increasing stakeholder consultation.

Linkages between National Single Window and Port Community Systems

Constraint

The foremost seaports in the region are gradually expanding their use of advanced information technology systems. Many BIMSTEC seaports have installed some forms of terminal operating system and container terminal management system, often by the container terminal operators who have introduced these systems as part of their concession arrangements. The next step is establishing port community systems. These link members of a port community in a similar way that national single windows link members of the trade facilitation community. Port community systems connect the diverse parties involved in port activities through a neutral and open electronic platform. This enables the secure exchange of information between public and private stakeholders, thereby improving the competitive position of various seaport community members. These systems optimize, manage, and automate port and logistics processes through the single submission of data, and they connect transport and logistics chains.

Port community systems enable the exchange of data between parties and give access in real-time to the status of consignments as they undergo various transactions between the arrival of goods at a port—by sea, in the case of imports and transshipments—and their exit by either sea or land and vice versa in the case of exports. Customs and/or national single windows should interface directly with port community systems as trade facilitation is a critical element in the efficiency of port logistics. India has a national system, Bangladesh has a system at Chattogram, and Hamburg Port Consulting has a contract to establish a port community system for Thailand. Both Myanmar and Sri Lanka are at the planning stage for such applications.

Strategy

BIMSTEC will encourage member states to advance national single windows and port community systems at the most important seaports and establish information and communications technology links between them.

Goals

All major BIMSTEC seaports should have port community systems or equivalents linked to national single windows by 2030 to enhance container tracking for stakeholders.

Component 4: Cooperation and Capacity Building

Within the next 10 years, the trade facilitation demands of the trading community are expected to change significantly, as are the responses of border agencies. The latter will involve the introduction of, or more widespread application of, advanced processing and procedures, supported by even higher levels of automation. The traditional roles and working practices of customs officers and other border officials will change appreciably. The nature of this change is difficult to predict, but looking at the experiences of countries with the most advanced trade facilitation conditions could be a useful guide. Change inherently raises the need for institutional and capacity-building programs to be able to implement new approaches to processing and procedures. This will involve not only technical training but also changes in mindsets and trust. Change management will inevitably be particularly difficult at remote land border posts and land ports.

Regional Cooperation

Constraint

BIMSTEC countries are also members of other regional initiatives, such as ASEAN and SAARC, as well as ADB's regional initiatives, namely, SASEC and GMS. While BIMSTEC has a clear regional cooperation remit, including for trade facilitation, it is important that cooperation initiatives under the BIMSTEC banner are compatible with those of these organizations to avoid duplication. BIMSTEC links the South Asia and Southeast Asia regions and it will be important that BIMSTEC connects with the programs of these organizations and initiatives to utilize their resources where appropriate. This linkage is likely to be invaluable in providing feedback to monitor progress in implementing the strategic framework.

Strategy

BIMSTEC encourages the active cooperation and support for other trade facilitation cooperation initiatives in the BIMSTEC region and may provide assistance where appropriate.

Goals

Active cooperation between regional trade facilitation initiatives, thereby ensuring overall compatibility and the elimination of possible duplication between programs.

Mutual Cooperation in Capacity-Building

Constraint

Trade facilitation conditions in BIMSTEC countries vary significantly. Thailand and India have the most advanced trade facilitation; Bangladesh and Sri Lanka less so; and Bhutan, Myanmar, and Nepal the least advanced, although they are making significant progress. These appreciable differences mean that the member countries also have different institutional and capacity-building needs. This suggests a more holistic approach is required for identifying the overall needs for capacity-building, without necessarily specifying in which particular area it is required. These differences could be turned into an advantage. BIMSTEC's more advanced countries could assist the less developed ones with institutional capacity-building. Skill transfer programs between authorities are commensurate with BIMSTEC's core mutual cooperation function. International funding institutions, as well as the WCO and WTO, could be resource providers.

Strategy

BIMSTEC will encourage exchanges between trade facilitation authorities in the member states based on mutual cooperation to assist in capacity-building and skill transfers.

Goals

Assistance in capacity-building through mutual cooperation between partner agencies, combined with additional support from the international funding institutions if deemed appropriate.

Internal Capacity-Building

Constraint

Enhancing trade facilitation will require skills upgrading and training in new techniques and technologies, particularly with the increased application of automated systems. Governments and international funding institutions have been assisting countries through customs computer system upgrades, the development of national single windows, and the design of trade information portals. This external assistance requires complementary internal capacity-building to ensure these applications are not only implemented successfully but are also self-sustaining. Without this capacity-building, investments in soft infrastructure will be put at risk.

Customs officers will need new skill sets to be able to deal with the inevitable increase in automation. It is essential that trained personnel in specialist areas are retained within the service. There is a concern in some BIMSTEC countries that staff rotation policies and government remuneration levels risk the loss of such personnel, particularly the computer staff, because of their specialist skills being marketable to the private sector. Staff retention will become an increasingly important focus in capacity-building programs to ensure that the benefits of these initiatives can be realized over longer periods. The focus on technical training should increasingly be based on train-the-trainer approaches to ensure the wider dispersal of knowledge throughout organizations.

Strategy

BIMSTEC will encourage the provision of internal capacity-building training to enhance the skills of personnel working on trade facilitation activities. Member states with advanced training capacities may provide training for personnel from other BIMSTEC countries.

Goals

Increased number of internal technical training courses for trade facilitation personnel to raise the overall level of professionalism within their organizations and their ability to implement advanced processing techniques.

Implementation and Monitoring

Guiding Principles

The strategic framework's implementation should be guided by the following seven principles:

- country ownership;
- results orientation, combined with pragmatism;
- flexibility and responsiveness to country needs;
- reform and modernization;
- active participation and involvement of the private sector;
- partnerships with development partners; and
- mutual cooperation.

Country Ownership

Successfully implementing the strategic framework will depend on the BIMSTEC Secretariat and each member state taking ownership of the initiative. The framework is essentially a country-driven program requiring the commitment not only of the government bodies responsible for various aspects of trade facilitation but also other national stakeholders representing the trading and transport communities.

Results Orientation Combined with Pragmatism

The strategic framework is focused on achieving realistic goals that are specific, measurable, attainable, relevant, and, in some cases, time-bound. Because member states are at significantly different stages of advancement in their trade facilitation situations, realizing goals will be easier for some countries than others, and national priorities may differ. The strategic framework is a pathway to achieve the overall goal by 2030, while recognizing that progress will take place at different speeds, reflecting individual situations and resource availability.

Flexibility and Responsiveness to Country Needs

The wide diversity in the economic development of BIMSTEC countries calls for a differentiated approach to the strategic framework's design based on multi-speed and multi-track implementation that reflects country contexts. Flexibility and responsiveness to the needs of member states will contribute significantly to realizing outcomes. Interventions may only involve a subset of the BIMSTEC countries to which the constraints being addressed apply, rather than necessarily to all member states.

Reform and Modernization

The strategic framework assumes all member states want to enhance their trade facilitation practices, gradually progressing toward the standards achieved in developed countries. Getting there will require institutional and operational reforms, combined with the adoption of new approaches balancing control, revenue generation, and facilitation, as well as embracing advanced methodologies and automation.

Participation and Involvement of the Private Sector

The private sector is an essential stakeholder in both trade and trade facilitation, and is often the chief demand driver for initiating change. The participation and involvement of these stakeholders will be vital for the effective implementation of trade facilitation initiatives and for advising on changes in demands emerging from altering trading conditions. Partnerships are needed with the private sector to enhance trade facilitation, be they in the form of service receivers or investors in hard or soft infrastructure. The active participation of the private sector in National Trade Facilitation Committees or their equivalents will be essential for enhancing trade facilitation.

Partnerships with Development Partners

The strategic framework can be a platform for mobilizing resources, not only from BIMSTEC governments but also from multilateral institutions and the private sector. There is recognition of the fact that some member states have limited fiscal and technical resources to enhance trade facilitation. Development partners can provide both financial and technical assistance to support trade facilitation initiatives. Coordinating this assistance will be important and the BIMSTEC's Secretariat supported by ADB and guided by member states should regularly coordinate with the bilateral and multilateral institutions that can play an important role in advancing trade facilitation in the region.

Mutual Cooperation

BIMSTEC is based on the principle of multisectoral technical and economic cooperation. It is assumed that this extends to cooperation within all sectors of interest, including trade facilitation. Such cooperation within BIMSTEC could extend to member states providing technical assistance or expertise and training if required and requested.

Resource Mobilization

Implementing the strategic framework will be funded using the internal resources of BIMSTEC countries, supplemented by available bilateral and multilateral resources. Multilateral institutions actively engaged in trade facilitation initiatives in the region in recent years include ADB, USAID, UNESCAP, WCO, and the World Bank. All have indicated their provisional commitment to providing financial and/or technical support for implementing elements of the framework if requested. These institutions can also help generate private sector interest and their participation in trade facilitation initiatives. The increased engagement of development partners can also enhance resource mobilization required for implementing elements of the strategic framework and assist the Secretariat in program coordination and monitoring if requested.

Progress Monitoring

The strategic framework is results-oriented. Each subcomponent has its own specific goal or goals that combine to realize the overall framework goal. An effective monitoring system must be established to measure progress in meeting the subcomponent goals.

There are two main options for monitoring the implementation of the strategic framework with subcomponent goals acting as performance indicators. The first is establishing through technical assistance a central monitoring body within BIMSTEC, possibly reporting directly to the Secretariat. Annual data could be provided by each country through their national trade facilitation committees or equivalent, collating information from national agencies. The second option would be for the BIMSTEC Trade Facilitation Working Group, currently engaged in finalizing the BIMSTEC Free Trade Area Agreement to take on this added responsibility and to report annually. It may also be possible to use the data compilation resources of partner trade facilitation initiatives.

A midterm review of the strategic framework should be considered in 2025 to take stock of the progress made and adjust the timing for achieving individual subcomponent goals if deemed appropriate. The volatility caused by the COVID-19 pandemic, high commodity prices, global inflation, and the Russian invasion of Ukraine will hopefully have passed by then, and normal trading activities will have resumed. The review could also be an opportunity to reappraise subcomponent strategies and goals in light of the subsequent events and market pressures encountered during the period up to 2025.

STATUS OF TRADE FACILITATION IN THE BAY OF BENGAL INITIATIVE FOR MULTI-SECTORAL TECHNICAL AND ECONOMIC COOPERATION (BIMSTEC)

This appendix looks at the state of each of the BIMSTEC country's trade facilitation situations and identifies some of the outstanding challenges, including whether member states have specific plans or strategies to address these constraints. Because BIMSTEC countries are at different stages of development, this information was needed to help formulate the planning of future development pathways. The objective was to establish the base situation from which the strategic framework will map out future progress and how individual country needs can be addressed within both national and regional contexts.

Bangladesh

Bangladesh has adopted a range of measures designed to facilitate trade. The country uses the Harmonized Commodity Description and Coding System of the WCO and the Automated System for Customs Data World (ASYCUDA World) in the National Board of Revenue, which is responsible for customs services. It has also signed a letter of intent to implement the WCO's SAFE Framework and joined the Revised Kyoto Convention on the Simplification and Harmonization of Customs (RKC). In September 2016, Bangladesh ratified the Trade Facilitation Agreement of the WTO; the agreement is the main framework for enhancing national trade facilitation. The Ministry of Commerce is the main implementing agency and has established the National Trade and Transport Facilitation Committee to manage the agreement's implementation.

Current Situation

The National Board of Revenue (NBR) drafted a new customs act in 2018 to replace a 1969 act. The new legislation is designed to accommodate the trade facilitation provisions of the RKC, the SAFE Framework, and the TFA and is focused on automation and the development of international best practices. The new act will cement existing amendments made to the 1969 law and the significant changes that have taken place within Bangladesh Customs since then. The new act has been approved by the Cabinet but needs to be submitted to and approved by the Parliament. It is understood that further modifications to the draft act may be required before its enactment.

Bangladesh Customs has updated its information technology systems by using the web-based ASYCUDA World, with funding from ADB. The system was first operated in Chattogram port in 2018 and is now used in six customs houses and 24 customs stations, including at all the main border crossings. It is gradually being extended to cover all land border stations and more links with the private sector. All customs declarations have to be made online into the system. Letters of credit and the checking and payment of duties can also be made through online links with banks.

The Bangladesh Trade Portal is the official source of all regulatory information to assist traders importing goods into Bangladesh or exporting to other countries. The Ministry of Commerce set up the portal to improve the predictability and transparency of the country's trading laws and processes. It is a one-stop point for information on trade requirements. Although it only advises traders on trade-related information, it is also a tool for the government and other stakeholders to reduce, modernize, and simplify regulations in line with international best practices.

The emphasis on infrastructure expansion specifically associated with trade facilitation has been on establishing the 23 land ports managed by the Bangladesh Land Port Authority. Most are along the border with India. These facilities are either operated directly by the authority or by the private sector on a build-operate-transfer basis. ADB has assisted in upgrading the Benapole land border complex and has undertaken feasibility studies on the land ports at Akhaura, Banglabandha, Burimari, Gobrakura-Koroitoli, Nakugoan, and Tamabil. At Chattogram, the port off-dock container freight stations have been developed to handle containers to be taken off the port for final clearance to help relieve congestion in the port's container terminals.

The National Trade and Transport Facilitation Committee's implementation of the TFA is seen as a national priority and is the main focus of trade facilitation in Bangladesh for further modernizing customs and, to a lesser extent, other border agencies. Table A1.1 shows the status of the agreement's implementation. The WTO estimates that this was 34.5% completed in January 2020.

Table A.1.1: Implementation Status of the Trade Facilitation Agreement in Bangladesh

Article	Description	Status
1.1–1.2	Publication	A/B: Laws, rules, regulations, and orders are available on the national trade portal of the Ministry of Commerce.
1.3	Enquiry points	C: National enquiry points established with customs. Sanitary, phytosanitary, and technical barriers to trade have their own enquiry points, rather than through the national portal.
2.1	Opportunity for comment and information	B: Ministry of Commerce and National Board of Revenue (NBR) facilitate feedback from government agencies, ministries, and departments.
2.2	Consultation	B: MOC and NBR consult with members of the trading community on changes in rules and regulations.
3	Advanced rulings	A: NBR introduced regulations to undertake advanced rulings, but other agencies do not have this arrangement.
4	Procedures for appeal	A/B: Customs procedures are in place, but other border agencies lack transparent appeal procedures.
5.1	Notification of advanced controls or inspections	B: No progress yet, as there is a need to revisit procedures to agree on unified procedures and coordination.
5.2	Detention	A: Customs has implemented changes and these will be included in the new customs act.
5.3	Test procedures	C: Comprehensive rules still need to be formulated on testing and inspection procedures.
6.1	Fees and charges	B: Fees and charges are published in the official gazette, but not in advance of changes being made.
6.2	Discipline on fees and charges	B: Customs fees and charges are based on services provided.
6.3	Penalty discipline	B: Rationalizing the penalties is completed, but they need to be included in the new customs act.

continued on next page

Table A.1.1 continued

7.1	Pre-arrival processing	C: Pre-arrival processing of import general manifest and bills of lading achieved with USAID/World Bank assistance, but no pre-arrival processing of declarations permitted.
7.2	Electronic payment	B: Automated System for Customs Data World interfaces with banks and there is an e-payment application.
7.3	Separation of release from the final determination	A: Customs have implemented a provisional assessment process.
7.4	Risk management	C: Customs have established risk management teams, but this has not been rolled out in all offices, thus not yet fully implemented. Other agencies lack risk management capability at this stage. World Bank/USAID is assisting.
7.5	Post-clearance auditing	C: Customs received training from ADB and USAID/World Bank on the system and transaction-based auditing, but the process is not yet fully implemented.
7.6	Average release times	A: Time-release studies were conducted at Chattogram port and Benapole land port. Further studies are planned.
7.7	Authorized economic operator (AEO)	C: Directive has been issued. Program planning with ADB and USAID assistance, but not fully implemented. Only three pharmaceutical companies have been awarded AEO status.
7.8	Expedited shipments	C: Special arrangements for couriers, but not for expedited shipments. USAID assisting in planning measures.
7.9	Perishable goods	C: No special arrangements, but normally given priority. Draft provisions have been developed with ADB for inclusion in the new customs act, but most perishable goods involve clearance by other agencies, and as yet no development partner has been found for such assistance.
8	Border agency cooperation	C: World Bank has agreed to fund a coordinated border management program; no development partner for cross-border agency cooperation.
9	Import under customs control	A: Implemented procedures for monitoring and supervision in place.
10.1	Formalities and documentation requirements	A/C: Some initial work undertaken by customs, but will need input from other border agencies. As yet no development partner.
10.2	Acceptance of copies	A/B: Implemented, but digital signatures are not yet permitted.
10.3	Use of international standards	A: Compliant with Revised Kyoto Convention on the Simplification ahd Harmonization of Customs (RKC), Standards to Secure and Facilitate Trade Framework, and Harmonized Commodity Description and Coding System.
10.4	Single window	C: Currently being implemented with World Bank, but further assistance is needed in implementation.
10.5	Pre-shipment Inspection	A/B: Inactive, but the Ministry of Commerce has a form of pre-shipment system on certain imports.
10.6	Use of customs brokers	A: Compliant. Importers and exporters use brokers; although not mandatory.
10.7	Common border procedures	A: Procedures are nominally the same at all border posts.
10.8	Rejected goods	A: Compliant with a clause in Customs Act.
10.9	Temporary admission	B: Provisions are in place, but need updating.
11	Freedom of transit	A/B/C: System in place, but requires cross-border motor agreement to be implemented and further infrastructure provided with either international funding institution aid or through domestic funding.
12	Customs cooperation	B: Compliant, but needs further cooperation with neighboring countries.
23	National Committee on Trade Facilitation	A: Compliant, through effectiveness in enforcing compliance with Trade Facilitation Agreement.

A = full implementation, B = part implementation, C = signifying that implementation will need external assistance

Sources: Asian Development Bank. 2019. *Borders without Barriers: Facilitating Trade in SASEC Countries.* Manila; latest status notification to World Trade Organization; Asian Development Bank.

Outstanding Concerns

While Bangladesh has made significant progress in enhancing trade facilitation, many NTBs still need to be addressed so that the country can provide a modern trade facilitation environment. The rankings in international surveys (Appendix II) show that trade facilitation is a constraint to trading activity. A special concern is the negative time and cost constraints apparent in the World Bank's Doing Business Survey.

The National Trade and Transport Facilitation Committee was formed in 2018; its core function was to implement the TFA. There are concerns over the committee's effectiveness in unifying the interests of all border agencies and its ability to coordinate with trade stakeholders. Its role is to define policies, procedures, roles, and responsibilities, but this appears to be in question since it has not come out with a short- to medium-term trade facilitation development strategy at this stage.

A unified platform for coordination among border agencies is lacking with each agency often acting independently, responding to their respective ministries. Agencies do not necessarily perceive border clearance as a cooperative effort involving customs and themselves working together as a team. Establishing the national single window should help to demonstrate the need for cooperation, provided these agencies can be linked to the system. It is needed to coordinate the interests of the border agencies in implementing one-stop processing.

The National Board of Revenue–Bangladesh Customs has a high level of automation through ASYCUDA World. The Border Guards Bangladesh has its own information and communication technology applications. Unfortunately, these levels of automation are not necessarily replicated in the case of other border agencies, many of which still rely on paper documentation. These parties need to upgrade their information technology capabilities to be able to issue certificates and authorize clearances online, as well as link into the national single window. Many of the longer clearance times in the ports and land ports are due to problems raised by these other agencies before the final clearance by customs.

The national single window is not yet operational but is being progressed with the assistance of the World Bank. It is anticipated it will eventually encompass 39 agencies and the private sector and enable the electronic exchange of data, electronic processing of declarations, and the streamlining of business processing. Not all 39 agencies have IT systems that can easily link up, so it may take time to develop and fully implement the single window. Connecting the main agencies needs to be prioritized with the latest date for full commissioning being 2024.

Bangladesh lacks an effective customs valuation database. The current database consists of valuations based on previous shipments with the same 8-digit harmonized system code held within the ASYCUDA system. The problem is there are significant differences in values for the same digit code—for example, a vehicle may have several different versions with different values, but the same harmonized system code. Another example is paper products that may have many different codes depending on their ultimate purpose, and because this coding is not an exact science, it is open to different interpretations. This results in frequent valuation disputes leading to protracted delays before the final agreement and release. The database needs to be updated and modified for it to be effective in these situations.

Bangladesh has only a few mutual recognition agreements with other countries. This means that foreign sanitary, phytosanitary, and trading standards certificates are not accepted by Bangladesh's border agencies for import shipments and that Bangladesh certificates are not accepted by export countries. Many of the longer import clearance delays are caused by having to retest shipments to get a Bangladesh certificate. Mutual recognition agreements are designed to eliminate these problems by their ability to have foreign certificates accepted on imports and exports. Having such an agreement with India will be critical because the country is one of Bangladesh's largest import partners.

As noted, sanitary, phytosanitary, and trading standards issues can be significant trade inhibitors. Internal studies by the Ministry of Commerce, with ADB assistance, have been done to synthesize sanitary, phytosanitary, and technical standards measures. These recommended actions were to establish a policy and regulatory framework, institutional strengthening, and strengthening of sanitary, phytosanitary, and trading standards infrastructure (laboratories, for example), and capacity-building. Unfortunately, these recommendations made in 2014 are still awaiting full implementation largely because of limited resources.

While modernizing border infrastructure is both required and ongoing, anecdotal evidence suggests the upgrading that has been completed has had only a limited impact on clearance times when compared to improvements in processing. The exception is the construction of inland clearance/container depots (ICDs) whose function is to clear container traffic inland, thus relieving port congestion—a serious issue at Chattogram port. Dhaka's ICD handled over 95,000 twenty-foot equivalent units in 2019, well beyond its original design capacity. Its high growth of late has been mainly due to the double-tracking of the rail line between Chattogram port and the Kamalapur facility. Despite the impact of COVID-19, the facility's storage limit of 4,267 twenty-foot equivalent units has been at capacity in 2021. Another ICD at Dhaka is urgently needed, and the government has suggested setting up a new one near the Dhirasram railway station attached to the Dhaka eastern bypass. Proposals were also made for another ICD near the Banglabandha western rail station and another in the Pubail area of the Gazipur district. None of these proposals have yet got to the implementation stage, though the Dhirasram option is now actively under discussion as a possible PPP with DP Ports.

Lack of capabilities and capacities are getting in the way of enhancing trade facilitation. Personnel across border agencies are not equally skilled. This is particularly apparent in trade facilitation and IT. More investment is needed in capacity-building workshops and technical assistance programs for border personnel to enable them to become trade facilitators rather than trade controllers. Staff rotation policies can also be a problem, as staff are trained in a particular skill and then transferred to other government organizations.

Bangladesh has no trade facilitation master plan at this stage that clearly identifies priorities and matches them with internal and external resources. In the short-term, it is clear that making progress on trade facilitation is mainly planned through the implementation of the TFA by the National Trade and Transport Facilitation Committee, but this does not include other border agencies, ministries, and organizations, such as seaport authorities. A coordinated national trade facilitation master plan is needed.

Bhutan

Bhutan's trade facilitation measures have been set out in the Five-Year Plan 2018–2022. These included developing trade infrastructure, establishing an export fund, and strengthening trade facilitation and automated systems. Bhutan signed the Revised Kyoto Convention on the Simplification and Harmonization of Customs (RKC) in 2014 and uses the WCO's Harmonized Commodity Description and Coding System. It was granted WTO observer status in 1998 and applied for membership in 1999. The country had reached an advanced stage of acceding to the WTO, but the accession process was suspended in 2008 due to the need for greater public debate and awareness. Bhutan remains the only BIMSTEC country that is not a World Trade Organization member.

Bhutan has no official body that specifically leads trade facilitation policy. The Department of Trade under the Ministry of Economic Affairs is nominally responsible for trade facilitation but this mandate is shared with the Department of Revenue and Customs, an agency under the Ministry of Finance.

Current Situation

A National Trade Facilitation Committee was formed in 2013 to coordinate government and private sector agencies in addressing legal and regulatory barriers to trade. Unfortunately, the committee had only limited success and was replaced in 2015 with the National Transport and Trade Facilitation Committee, whose remit was extended to include transport. Meetings have been held, but the position, authority, and enforcement powers of its secretariat remain unclear. It is currently housed in the Department of Revenue and Customs. The Better Business Council was set up in 2018 to promote dialogue between the public and private sectors and its remit also included discussion on trade-related matters.

The published strategy of the Customs and Excise Division of the Department of Revenue and Customs is to:

* simplify and streamline customs procedures;
* provide efficient services to importers, exporters, and taxpayers;
* facilitate speedy and smooth customs clearance by applying risk management;
* create public awareness and encourage tax compliance;
* levy the correct amount of tax and duties;
* implement laws, rules, and regulations uniformly;
* prevent the import and export of restricted and prohibited goods; and
* supply international trade information (such as reliable, timely, and comprehensive statistics on import and export, and trade and travel).

A new customs act and its implementing rules and regulations came into force in 2017. These are considered to comply with the RKC and international best practices, including the examination of the provisions of transit rights, harmonization of documentation and procedures, and integration of cross-border facilities, as well as making progress on paperless trading.

The other main parties involved in trade facilitation are the Agriculture and Food Regulatory Authority, which is responsible for sanitary and phytosanitary matters, and the Standards Bureau, which takes care of product standards. Bhutan has a sanitary and phytosanitary laboratory and sub-offices in all districts that can issue certificates for import and export shipments, but these are not always accepted by other countries due to the lack of accreditation standards. The Standards Bureau is in a similar position for the certification of export products.

One of the reasons for the variations in the international performance surveys discussed in Appendix II may be that shipments from India are treated differently from those from other countries, resulting in expedited clearances of Indian traffic. The latest bilateral agreement, signed in 2016, means the two countries have free trade (i.e., no tariff barriers) and their currencies are at par. Some 91% of Bhutan's exports and 84% of imports are with India. These shipments are entered separately into the Bhutan Automated Customs System and inspected with clearance achieved in under 2 hours unless it is a complex mixed load. Non-Indian imports, however, are sent to the ICD or Customs House for clearance, and final release can sometimes only be secured after more than a day.

Bhutan has signed the Bangladesh-Bhutan-India-Nepal Motor Vehicle Agreement, but its implementation has not yet been ratified because of concerns over environmental damage if larger Indian vehicles were permitted and because of a weight restriction on trucks traveling inland. A steep mountain climb immediately to the north of Phuentsholing means most import traffic for inland delivery has to be transferred from Indian to Bhutanese trucks, with resultant delays in transshipment and the need to reweight the vehicles traveling inland.

Table A.1.2 assess for comparative purposes Bhutan's situation on the theoretical basis that it was a WTO member and also a Trade Facilitation Agreement signatory. The table gives an indication of implementation priorities, which can help identify the main measures needed to tackle trade facilitation in a regional strategic context.

Table A.1.2: Prioritization of Trade Facilitation Agreement Articles for Reform in Bhutan

Article	Description	Status
1.1–1.2	Publication	Medium: Pre-feasibility study of a trade portal completed, but portal not yet implemented.
1.3	Enquiry points	Medium: Enquiry points exist, but not in a form that represents a consolidated trade enquiry point. Each agency has to be contacted separately.
2.1	Opportunity for comment and information	Low: Not applicable at this stage, as not a World Trade Organization (WTO) member.
2.2	Consultation	Medium: Not applicable until the membership of the WTO is agreed upon.
3	Advanced rulings	High: Not being applied.
4	Procedures for appeal	Medium: Procedure present.
5.1	Notification of advanced Controls or inspections	Medium: Not applied.
5.2	Detention	Medium: Some rules applied.
5.3	Test procedures	Medium: Some procedures applied, but not to Trade Facilitation Agreement levels. Limited availability of testing resources.
6.1	Fees and charges	Probably compliant.

continued on next page

Table A.1.2 continued

Article	Description	Status
6.2	Discipline on fees and charges	Probably not fully compliant.
6.3	Penalty discipline	High: Probably not fully compliant at this stage.
7.1	Pre-arrival processing	Medium: Not implemented and difficult to do so on cross-border trade due to limited transit times, although possible on imports through Indian ports.
7.2	Electronic payment	High: Duties can be paid electronically through Bhutan Automated Customs System.
7.3	Separation of release from the final determination	Medium: Believed to be implemented.
7.4	Risk management	High: Not fully implemented with no risk management module in Bhutan Automated Customs System.
7.5	Post-clearance audit	High: No system in place.
7.6	Average release time	Medium: Time-release study at Phuentsholing by UNESCAP. Customs have customer service delivery standards in place.
7.7	Authorized economic operator	High: No system in place.
7.8	Expedited shipments	Medium: No system in place.
7.9	Perishable goods	High: No system in place, but perishables are usually given priority
8	Border agency cooperation	High: Cooperation mechanism not yet in place
9	Import under customs control	Low: Import movements, including transit from Phuentsholing to other crossings via India, nominally under customs control in convoys. Goods in transit systems for traffic routed via Kolkata port, but again this is under Indian controls.
10.1	Formalities and documentation requirements	High: Not implemented further work needed.
10.2	Acceptance of copies	Medium: Originals are usually required at some stage in the clearance process.
10.3	Use of international standards	High: Further implementation required.
10.4	Single window	High: Pre-feasibility study completed and National Transport and Trade Facilitation Committee promoting national single window, but no progress at this stage.
10.5	Pre-shipment inspection	Low: Not relevant to short-distance transit goods.
10.6	Use of customs brokers	Medium: Compliant as customs brokers present.
10.7	Common border procedures	High: Not implemented as cooperation between agencies remains an issue.
10.8	Rejected goods	Medium: System in place, but might require revision to comply.
10.9	Temporary admission	High: System in place, but might require revision to comply.
11	Freedom of transit	High: Some transit measures are in place for inland movements and to other border crossings.
12	Customs cooperation	High: Problem in establishing customs cooperation, other than through the SAARC and SASEC.
23	National Committee on Trade Facilitation	High: National Transport and Trade Facilitation Committee formed, but with limited powers.

Sources: Asian Development Bank. 2019. *Borders without Barriers: Facilitating Trade in SASEC Countries*. Manila; Asian Development Bank.

Outstanding Concerns

The Bhutan Automated Customs System was principally oriented toward national taxation when it was launched in 2002, with customs applications being integrated into the system. It has nine modules for import, export, transit, and payments and has undergone three upgrades since its launch. Its limitations are that it is not web-based, connected with other government offices, cannot support an NSW, and lacks a risk management module. A modern replacement was needed. With ADB funding, establishing the Revenue Administration and Management Information System (RAMIS) as a replacement in two stages was proposed. Stage one (RAMIS I) was for direct and sales tax modules for the Department of Revenue.

RAMIS II was to be the parallel customs system. The customs and excise modules were expected to be completed by the end of October 2015 and January 2016, respectively. In October 2015 it was decided to temporarily suspend work on RAMIS II but it was restarted in April 2017 after RAMIS I was stabilized. A second system audit was conducted in 2017 and the various deficiencies in RAMIS II were identified resulting in the Department of Revenue deciding to discontinue its development. As a result, the original Bhutan Automated Customs System (BACS) remains in place, although it now only covers customs, as the tax component is now handled separately by RAMIS I. BACS is a stand-alone devolved system, relying on a central server with local servers at border posts updating the central server daily. Unfortunately, the system cannot be linked to other agencies or be used as a future core component of an NSW in its current form. It also tends to function as a mechanism to record transactions rather than acting as a processing system, with clearances still being reliant on a combination of manual and paper-based transactions.

Bhutan faces significant sanitary and phytosanitary constraints because the Agriculture and Food Regulatory Authority lacks the physical and human resources to process import and export shipments efficiently. Samples have to be sent from the border offices to the national laboratory for testing, but the scope of these tests is limited and insufficient for science-based risk analysis. The authority has no web-based application to issue certificates online or to disseminate information back to the border. The lack of accreditation and mutual recognition agreements is a particular problem concerning exports of agricultural produce.

The condition of border infrastructure, along with transport infrastructure in general, is a constraint to improving the country's trade facilitation environment. Some 74% of all trade passes through the Phuentsholing border crossing. Inbound cargoes from India are processed at the border post and a mini dry port funded by ADB (81%) and the Government of Bhutan (19%) under a SASEC program. The port built on 5.4 acres of land can house up to 48 trucks, handle the unloading of container traffic, and process customs clearances. A 15-acre site has also been allocated at the nearby Pasakha Industrial Estate for constructing an ICD. This will divert much of the heavy transport serving the estate, particularly the ferrosilicon trucks passing through Phuentsholing crossing. The building has started with funding support from the Government of India.

Capacity-building is critical for modernizing Bhutan's trade facilitation environment. Yet, this is particularly difficult in a small country with limited human and financial resources, making in-house professional and technical training all the more needed if Bhutan is to meet its trade facilitation aspirations. While external funding may be available, human resources and low staff turnover is needed for external training programs to be successful. Studies by United Nations Economic and Social

Commission for Asia and the Pacific and ADB in 2017 identified both short- and long-term measures required to transform trade facilitation. These were:

Short-Term

- Implementing online application and approval, issuance, and renewal of licenses, certificates, and permits for a number of similar processes among government organizations, and between government organizations and stakeholders;
- Establishing the electronic exchange of documents between customs departments in Bangladesh, Bhutan, and India for transit clearance in India;
- Rearranging the internal workflows of regional revenue and customs offices; and
- Strengthening professional relationships among all parties in the trade process.

Longer-Term

- Launching a national single window;
- Ensuring legal consistency for the introduction of an NSW and electronic procedures;
- Ensuring transparency in legal, policy, and procedural requirements;
- Establishing authorized economic operator and trusted trader programs;
- Upgrading the skills of frontline officials, including in information and communication technology, to support the implementation of modern tools; and
- Improving transport and border crossing infrastructure.

While some progress has been achieved in expediting transit traffic between Kolkata/Haldia and Phuentsholing and improvements made in border infrastructure, many of these proposed measures still represent a work in progress. While border delays are not yet at critical levels as trading volumes are comparatively low, this is not expected to be the case in the longer term, as the Bhutanese economy grows and the benefits of the investments in hydro schemes filter through.

India

As a member of the WCO and WTO, India has adopted many of the international conventions and agreements covering trade facilitation. These include:

- WTO Trade Facilitation Agreement;
- Revised Kyoto Convention;
- International Convention on Harmonized Commodity Description and Coding System
- Customs Convention on the Admission Temporaire/Temporary Admission (ATA) Carnet for Temporary Admission of Goods;
- WCO SAFE Framework;
- Transport International Routiere Convention; and
- International Convention on Mutual Administrative Assistance for the Prevention, Investigation and Repression of Customs Offences.

The Central Board of Indirect Taxes and Customs is the customs administration agency and the apex body for enhancing trade facilitation.

Current Situation

The main emphasis on advancing trade facilitation has tended to focus on improving the performance of trade coming through seaports. This is natural since over 90% of India's trade is carried by sea to and from its global markets. Trade with Bangladesh, Bhutan, and Nepal across land borders is important to these countries, but it is of much less importance to India's overall trade activity. That said, India's efforts to improve trade facilitation have gradually spread to the land borders. A good example of this is the automation at customs. Here, trialing and implementation initially started at seaports and later were rolled out at the larger land borders.

The Indian Customs Electronic Data Exchange System (ICES) was introduced in 1995 as an approach to exchange and transact customs clearance information. ICES, through its Indian Customs Electronic Gateway (ICEGATE), operates at 252 customs locations and processes 99% of India's international trade. The system has been expanded and is now linked to 15 other parties using electronic data interchange. The Central Board of Indirect Taxes and Customs has established an e-storage and computerized handling system for indirect tax documents, called e-SANCHIT, which can be accessed via the Indian Customs Electronic Gateway. Through this mechanism, importers and exporters or their agents can download customs declarations and supporting documents, and carriers can enter their manifests and submit them with digital signatures. Some 97% of import/export declarations and manifests are now filed using these applications, with the remainder using approved service centers.

In 2016, India launched its national single window, described as the Single Window Interface for Facilitating Trade (SWIFT). This development enabled importers and exporters to link up with the Indian Customs Electronic Gateway and use integrated documentation. The previous system required nine different forms, which are now consolidated into a single form that can be distributed to six agencies. The system automatically identifies goods requiring clearance by other agencies and provides online clearances from them. The application files declarations and routes them to relevant agencies based on the harmonized system code, country of origin, and value; it then combines any decisions on these declarations into a centralized verdict on whether to release the goods online or not. SWIFT is also linked to the risk management module, thus reducing the levels of physical examination.

Indian customs have a fully operational risk management module within ICES that categorizes consignments based on their compliance risk. There are three main categories - shipments to be cleared without physical checks or the documentation needs further scrutiny before a decision on whether a physical examination is required or the shipment needs examining before the final clearance. Over 70% of trade is estimated to be exempt from a physical examination. This risk management application or "channeling" conforms with that used in countries with more advanced trade facilitation conditions.

A trade portal commissioned by the Ministry of Commerce is being run by the Federation of Indian Export Organizations. The portal, however, is principally oriented toward exports, as it is a tool for businesses to search, select, and contact Indian suppliers. Thus, it is more of a trade promotion application rather than a trade portal in the conventional sense since it does not as yet include import trade. The Central Board of Indirect Taxes and Customs has established a compliance information portal that provides information on the laws, procedures, customs acts, and partner government agencies responsible for regulating imports and exports of commodities.

Indian customs operate an AEO program under the SAFE Framework. Firms or traders are scrutinized by customs officials for compliance with supply-chain security and legal standards. Traders are granted AEO status, providing that they meet these standards. These entities are classified into three tiers, with 1 being the lowest. These tiers offer increasingly beneficial facilitation arrangements, thereby enabling faster clearances with only minimal periodic examinations to ensure the continued compliance of AEOs.

Congestion at container terminals is a considerable constraint at Indian ports, principally due to high dwell times between a container's arrival and landside delivery. The initial strategy to alleviate this situation was to set up CFSs around ports where shipments could be forwarded for clearance. Unlike conventional CFSs, where only less-than-containerload traffic is unstuffed, full containerload shipments were also mandated to be sent to these facilities for final clearance. This procedure raised extra costs for full container load importers, thereby limiting the benefits inherent in the risk management and AEO programs. To fix this problem, approved full containerload shipments can be collected by importers direct from terminals without routing via a CFS. This 2017-initiated approach not only reduces costs for importers but also ensures more rapid clearance from terminals.

Customs have made a major effort to standardize and simplify the documentation required for import/export clearance. In principle, only three mandatory documents are required: an electronic declaration, a commercial invoice or packing list, and a bill of lading or airway bill. Depending on the commodity and nature of the transaction, additional documents may be required. Anecdotal evidence suggests this is more often the case, particularly at land borders where risk management and AEOs are less prevalent.

The government recognizes the need to enhance trade facilitation in response to its ratification of the TFA and its relatively low ranking in the World Bank's Doing Business surveys. It has established the National Committee on Trade Facilitation, which has a three-tier structure: the committee chaired by a Cabinet secretary, a steering committee co-chaired by Revenue and Commerce secretaries, and ad hoc working groups to assist in specific provisions. The committee, which has 24 members representing departments or ministries monitors the implementation of the TFA. The steering committee is the operational arm responsible for identifying needed legislative changes and undertakes diagnostic work to ensure the agreement is eventually implemented in full.

Table A.1.3 estimates the compliance levels with the agreement, including for the implementation categories. India's compliance level with the agreement in 2021 was 78.2%, with Category A at 72.3% and Category B at 27.7%. Many Category B commitments due by 2022 were met before the original deadlines and were reported to the WTO in October 2020.

Table A.1.3: Implementation Status of the Trade Facilitation Agreement in India

Article	Description	Status
1.1	Publication	A/B: Mainly compliant as customs have a website covering trade procedures and costs, but not duties payable. Other border agencies generally lack comparable websites.
1.2	Information available through the Internet	A/B: Generally compliant, but does not indicate contacts at this stage.
1.3	Enquiry points	B: Trade portal only covers exports and has no Q&A capability.
1.4	Notification	B: Not yet compliant, but planned.
2.1	Opportunity for comment and information	A/B: Generally compliant, but further consultation ongoing.
2.2	Consultation	A: Compliant.
3	Advanced rulings	A/B: Generally compliant, as an advanced ruling process is in place.
4	Procedures for appeal	A/B: Procedures are in place, but further implementation is needed.
5.1	Notification of advanced controls or inspections	A/B: Mainly compliant, but some sanitary and phytosanitary aspects are not yet compliant.
5.2	Detention	A: Compliant with a system in place.
5.3	Test procedures	A: Compliant, but some testing constraints remain, particularly at land borders.
6.1	Fees and charges	A: Compliant with fees and charges published.
6.2	Discipline on fees and charges	A: Compliant.
6.3	Penalty discipline	A/B: Compliant, but part not yet accepted.
7.1	Pre-arrival processing	A/B Compliant, but some electronic pre-arrival data is not yet acceptable for processing.
7.2	Electronic payment	A: Compliant as a system in place.
7.3	Separation of release from the final determination	B: Partially implemented, especially for authorized economic operators (AEOs).
7.4	Risk management	B: Compliant, but probably requires more AEOs.
7.5	Post clearance audit	A: Mainly compliant, but some importers are reticent to use the system because of the risk of additional payments after the goods are sold.
7.6	Average release times	A: Compliant with time-release studies undertaken, though results not necessarily publicly available.
7.7	Authorized economic operator	A: AEO scheme operating, although may need significantly expanding.
7.8	Expedited shipments	A/B: Partly implemented, but some constraints are still outstanding.
7.9	Perishable goods	A/B: Perishable goods get priority. Issuing of letters indicating delays not yet implemented.
8	Border agency cooperation	A/B: Compliant, but some procedures and formalities are not aligned.
9	Import under customs control	A: Compliant with bonding and similar systems implemented.
10.1	Formalities and documentation requirements	A: Generally compliant.
10.2	Acceptance of copies	A/B: Generally compliant, but not all agencies accept copies and so some original hard copy documentation is still needed.

continued on next page

Table A.1.3 continued

Article	Description	Status
10.3	Use of international standards	A: International standards implemented wherever possible.
10.4	Single window	A: Single Window Interface for Facilitating Trade implemented, but not yet connected to all agencies.
10.5	Pre-shipment inspection	A/B: Generally compliant, but the application is not necessarily consistent between agencies.
10.6	Use of customs brokers	A: Compliant with extensive use of customs house brokers.
10.7	Common border procedures	A: Compliant with common procedures at all borders.
10.8	Rejected goods	A/B: Generally compliant, but not addressed consistently when rejected by sanitary and phytosanitary authorities.
10.9	Temporary admission	A/B: Compliant except for some inward and outward processing.
11	Freedom of transit	A/B: Compliant, but there are transit fees and there are also some problems in notifying close of transit movements.
12	Customs cooperation	A: Generally compliant.
23	National Committee on Trade Facilitation	A: National Committee on Trade Facilitation established.

A = full implementation, B = part implementation, C = signifying that implementation will need external assistance.

Sources: Asian Development Bank. 2019. *Borders without Barriers: Facilitating Trade in SASEC Countries*; 8 October 2020 notification to the World Trade Organization; Asian Development Bank.

Outstanding Concerns

Despite significant improvements in trade facilitation in the last 15 years, India still has nontariff barriers that adversely affect its rankings in international surveys, with India often being ranked below Thailand.

Modernizing border infrastructure remains a residual issue, despite improvements in ICPs at the Bangladesh and Nepal borders. These extensive facilities on the Indian side have addressed the issue of parking issues at the previous border posts, although in general, the problems tend to be on the other side of the border given the trade imbalances. The trend to address this situation has been to build ICPs on greenfield sites, bypassing congested border towns. Significant problems, however, have arisen in connecting these sites to the adjacent road networks, particularly due to land acquisition issues. This has delayed the implementation of the ICP program with some ICPs still under construction. While India is also funding ICPs on the Nepal side, this is not the case in Bangladesh or Myanmar. The Land Port Authority was set up to coordinate ICP activities and is responsible for their maintenance.

Efficient port facilitation is critical for India given its reliance on its seaports for international trade. Appreciable progress has been made in the customs arena, but there are many other players, including other border agencies and those in port logistics. Dwell times are still too high at many Indian ports by international standards. Shipping lines, their port agents, the port authority, and stevedores tend to work in isolation in terms of procedures and documentation requirements. Port community systems (PCSs) are designed to address this by linking all parties electronically, similar to a national single window. India has been a latecomer to the PCS concept and the rollout of the national system has been problematic. It has had to be redesigned and has been marred by software problems. The PCS has also failed to address some of the broader stakeholder concerns over data security.

As noted earlier, progress with customs procedures and processes has been largely achieved, but more needs to be done if the expected benefits are to be reaped. For example, the AEO program only has a relatively small percentage of overall importers/exporters, and traders are wary of the post-audit system whereby the audit may identify the need for increased duty payments after the goods have been sold. In principle, only three documents are required for a clearance; but in practice, more is required. A World Bank survey shows that Mumbai seaport in 2018 needed 10 documents to import and six to export.

ICES was initially connected to seaports and then spread to land borders and land customs stations. Some minor borders and land customs stations are still not online, though 245 stations have now been connected. A concern is the ability of other border agencies to fully participate in this automation process. Although the Single Window Interface for Facilitating Trade has been a significant step forward, this only fully covers seven agencies.

Sanitary, phytosanitary, and other agencies responsible for compliance with national trading standards have not modernized their automated processes to the same extent as customs. Traders often find it difficult to process all the requirements online, and the trade portal only covers exports. Procedures have also not been fully updated and consistent risk management is not yet in place. For sanitary and phytosanitary controls, in particular, testing laboratories near land borders are lacking, and as a result samples have to be sent to inland laboratories several days away, while the goods are held at the border. This is especially a problem for perishable goods, which may spoil before final sanitary or phytosanitary clearance is given. The difficulties encountered in establishing testing facilities and getting qualified personnel at remote border locations may mean that consolidation is required, whereby imports requiring sanitary and phytosanitary testing may only enter through designated border posts. The private sector could help alleviate this problem by setting up approved test facilities.

India recognizes its trade facilitation practices need to further improve to support its export trade and to efficiently handle imports for its growing economy. The National Trade Facilitation Action Plan contains specific activities designed to minimize NTBs. This included moving toward a "TFA+" that takes into consideration that the WTO's Trade Facilitation Agreement is merely a building block for improving trade facilitation and that further progress will be needed if India is to achieve its trade facilitation goals. The National Trade Facilitation Action Plan's objectives are improving India's Ease of Doing Business rankings by reducing transaction costs and times, reducing cargo release times, promoting a paperless regulatory environment, developing a transparent and predictable legal regime, and building better infrastructure to improve trade facilitation. The implementation strategy revolves around the following four pillars:

- Transparency to improve access to accurate and complete information;
- Greater use of technology to ease trade bottlenecks and improve efficiency;
- Simplification of procedures and risk-based assessments through simplified, uniform, and harmonized procedures and the increased adoption of a risk-based approach; and
- Infrastructure augmentation at customs stations (seaports, airports, land ports, land customs stations, and the road and rail infrastructure connecting customs stations).

The plan's circular contains a comprehensive 76-point action plan outlining specific actions to be taken, the agencies responsible for carrying them out, and the timeframes for implementation. For 2020–2023, a new action plan is being prepared with a vision to undertake additional reforms to bolster trade facilitation efforts and transform the cross-border clearance system by promoting efficient, transparent, risk-based, coordinated, digital, seamless, and technology-driven procedures, supported by infrastructure enhancement.

Myanmar

The government recognizes two multilateral agreements reflecting best practices in trade facilitation: the RKC and the Trade Facilitation Agreement. Myanmar became the 123rd signatory to the convention, which came into force in the country on 2 January 2021. Myanmar has indicated its intention to implement the SAFE Framework. It is also a signatory to the International Convention on the Harmonized Commodities Description and Coding System. The basic rules governing food safety, and animal and plant health standards are covered by the WTO Agreement on the Application of Sanitary and Phytosanitary Measures, and the government recognizes the WTO Technical Barriers to Trade Agreement.

The National Committee for Trade Facilitation is mainly led by two ministries: the Ministry of Commerce, particularly through the Department of Trade, and the Ministry of Planning and Finance, particularly through Myanmar Customs.

Current Situation

The stated vision of Myanmar Customs is to create a customs service that both facilitates international trade and makes it secure and protects social well-being and trade partnerships with stakeholders. Its stated mission is to facilitate trade by simplifying customs procedures while ensuring that customs revenue is properly collected. The objectives in meeting this mission are:

- Enhancing revenue collection by promoting trade;
- Preventing the loss of revenue and duties being evaded by effective control measures;
- Collecting data for the compilation of statistics on international trade;
- Modernizing and standardizing customs procedures with international practices;
- Cooperating and coordinating with allied law enforcement agencies; and
- Promoting the department's public image by enhancing the integrity of its personnel.

The initial emphasis appears to be on control rather than facilitation. This is reinforced by the stated roles and functions of Myanmar Customs to (i) examine and monitor imports/exports; (ii) examine passengers and their baggage entering or leaving Myanmar' (iii) assess and levy duties and taxes; (iv) enforce the Sea Customs Act, Land Customs Act, Tariff Law, and other related laws and regulations; (v) combat commercial fraud; and (vi) ensure that all goods entering or leaving Myanmar are correctly declared in conformity with applicable laws and procedures of the customs duties.

The Myanmar Customs IT processing application - the Myanmar Automated Cargo Clearance System - was implemented in November 2016 at customs headquarters. The system is based on the Japanese model for customs processing using IT and was set up with technical assistance and funding from Japan. The system encountered several difficulties after its initial roll-out at seaports and border stations. Since the system was implemented, customs clearance processes have not appeared to have become appreciably faster. To register in the system, traders or their representatives need to be physically present at the customs office to fill in and submit the registration form. The system is linked to the Ministry of Commerce, the port authority, the Food and Drug Administration, plant and animal quarantine agencies, the Department of Fisheries, and the Myanmar Economic Bank.

The Myanmar Automated Cargo Clearance System was expected to significantly reduce manual document checking through its automated document verification process (reviewing information, valuing goods, and the electronic payment of import duties). It was also expected the system would lead to the introduction of risk management for cargo inspection and the capability to track cargoes during the customs clearance and inspection processes. Anecdotal information suggests it has yet to fully achieve these goals. System upgrades were intended to reduce the need for signing hard copy documentation by other government agencies by the end of 2020.

The Myanmar Trade Portal is the single-stop point for all information on imports and exports requirements. It was set up by the Ministry of Commerce, which operates the portal on behalf of government agencies involved in the import/export process. From the portal, traders can obtain information on regulatory requirements. In some instances, the portal advises where to access information from the websites of other ministries but is not directly connected to these websites.

The National Committee for Trade Facilitation was formed in December 2016 in compliance with the requirements of the TFA, and the committee was restructured in 2017. It is chaired by the deputy commerce minister and jointly chaired by the deputy planning and finance minister. The committee has four working groups: communication and transparency, led by the Department of Trade; risk management, led by the Myanmar Customs; the single window, also led by customs; and test procedures, led by the Department of Consumer Affairs. The committee monitors progress in the country's compliance with the TFA using the self-assessment tools provided by the World Bank.

The National Single Window Blueprint was planned with the assistance of the World Bank as an initial work plan for implementing an NSW in December 2018, and ministerial approval was given to proceed. Under article 10.7 of the Trade Facilitation Agreement, the Single Window Group and the National Committee of Trade Facilitation requested third-party renting for technical assistance. Although there is a technical working group, it has as yet no private sector stakeholders on it. Myanmar joined the Live Operation for the Exchange of ASEAN Customs Declaration Documents on the 31st December 2020. USAID consultants have recommended a three-phase approach for establishing the NSW. The first is to develop the basic functionality within the certificate-of-origin issuing authority of the Ministry of Commerce's e-certificate-of-origin system to be able to send out e-Form D. The AXWAY Gateway and NSW routing platform have been set up and tested. In December 2019, Myanmar started participating in the ASEAN Single Window Live Operation after linking the country of the original certificate with ASEAN nations. The work for including electronic sanitary and phytosanitary data is underway.

The soft launch of the TradeNet 2.0 computerized import and export licensing module in January 2021 further enhanced the automation of licensing to facilitate trade. Its current utilization is 70% of total license issuance. Ten types of certificates-of-origin can also be obtained through the TradeNet online application system. Customs undertook time-release studies at some borders in 2019 and the results have been published on its website.

Despite the progress achieved in automation, Myanmar has only implemented 5.5% of the Trade Facilitation Agreement, according to the WTO (Table A.1.4).

Table A.1.4: Implementation Status of the Trade Facilitation Agreement in Myanmar

Article	Description	Status
1.1	Publication	C: Information published, but not always in advance of changes.
1.2	Information available through the internet	C: Trade portal provides trade information and indicates links to other ministries, but is not a centralized information repository.
1.3	Enquiry points	B: Enquiry points in various ministry websites, but no centralized point. Scheduled for implementation end-2025.
1.4	Notification	C: Notifications provided, but not necessarily in advance.
2.1	Opportunity for comment and information before coming into force	C: No effective mechanism in place.
2.2	Consultation	C: No effective mechanism in place.
3	Advanced rulings	C: System in place, but indications are that such rulings are difficult to obtain. Changes are almost completed.
4	Procedures for appeal	A: System in place.
5.1	Notification of advanced controls or inspections	C: Information not usually indicated in advance.
5.2	Detention	B: System in place, but not fully compliant. Scheduled for implementation end-2022.
5.3	Test procedures	C: Limited testing facilities.
6.1	Fees and charges	B: Fees and charges are fixed for most services. Scheduled for implementation end 2025.
6.2	Discipline on fees and charges	A: System in place, but required some changes and almost completed.
6.3	Penalty discipline	B: System in place, but needs adjusting to being fully compliant. Scheduled for implementation end 2025.
7.1	Pre-arrival processing	C: Preliminary declaration function in place in the automated system for pre-arrival processing.
7.2	Electronic payment	C: Payments are mainly using a system of deposits ahead of full e-payment applications. Customs are implementing a fully-electronic payment gateway with private banks.
7.3	Separation of release from the final determination	C: Under review.
7.4	Risk management	C: Risk management module in Myanmar Automated Cargo Clearance System, but other border agencies do not have matching applications/practices.
7.5	Post clearance audit	C: Application still under development, but almost completed.
7.6	Average release-times	C: Time-release studies were conducted in 2019 with ADB assistance and submitted to the Economic Research Institute for the Association of Southeast Asian Nations (ASEAN) via the ASEAN Secretariat in May 2020. Due to COVID-19, customs were unable to upload the results onto their website until 2021.

continued on next page

Table A.1.4 continued

Article	Description	Status
7.7	Authorized economic operator	C: Program was initiated in December 2017 with ADB assistance, but indications are that the number of AEOs is small.
7.8	Expedited shipments	C: No structured system in place.
7.9	Perishable goods	C: No structured system in place, but perishables usually receive priority.
8	Border agency cooperation	C: No formal structure in place.
9	Movement of goods under customs control intended for import	C: No formal structure in place, movements from port to inland clearance/container depots permitted.
10.1	Formalities and documentation requirements	C: Minimal reduction in documentation and procedures so far.
10.2	Acceptance of copies	C: The system accepts electronic copies but originals need to be submitted to customs on request.
10.3	Use of international standards	C: Revised Kyoto Convention and Trade Facility Agreement are regarded as guidelines for international best practices, as Myanmar is a signatory to both agreements.
10.4	Single window	C: A blueprint for the system is being developed with the World Bank. The custom system can be linked to the Single Window and can undertake the exchange of ATIGA e-form D and the ASEAN Customs Declaration Department with other countries
10.5	Pre-shipment inspection	A: System in place, but required changes that are almost completed.
10.6	Use of customs brokers	B: Customs brokers are usually present. Scheduled for full implementation end 2025.
10.7	Common border procedures and uniform documentation requirements	C: Further action is required to be compliant.
10.8	Rejected goods	B: System in place, but needs modification to be fully compliant. Scheduled for implementation end 2025.
10.9	Temporary admission	C: Systems need further development.
11	Freedom of transit	C: Clearances only permitted at border/port or ICD.
12	Customs cooperation	C: Participation in ASEAN, Greater Mekong Subregion, and South Asia Subregional Economic Cooperation meetings.
23	National Committee on Trade Facilitation	A: Formed, but no published material on committee participation and forward strategy.

A = full implementation, B = part implementation, C = signifying that implementation will need external assistance

Sources: World Trade Organization Database; Trade Facilitation Agreement notification; author's assessment.

Outstanding Concerns

Imports of goods into and exports from Myanmar are governed by the Sea Customs Act of 1878 and its 1956, 1959, 2015, and 2018 amendments, the Land Customs Act of 1924, the Export and Import Law of 2012, and the Tariff Law of 1992. These laws are administered by the Ministry of Planning and Finance, Myanmar Customs, and the Ministry of Commerce. Since they were passed, the country's trade facilitation situation has changed significantly. These laws must not impede progress in implementing the TFA, the modernization recommendations in the RKC, and the move toward paperless trading.

Myanmar recognizes that international best practices in trade facilitation are based on compliance with the agreement and the convention. Myanmar has a low implementation of Category A (5.5%) items and a high number of Category C ones (85.3%). It may be that since last reported to the WTO greater compliance may have taken place or is underway, such that some Category C items are moving toward B or even A.

The Myanmar Automated Cargo Clearance System is being upgraded, migrating from the WCO Data Model 2 to 3.7. Myanmar Customs has waived the need for submitting original commercial documents by accepting electronic Form-D in the Myanmar Automated Cargo Clearance System since April 2020. The system's risk management module provides for channeling, but the level of green channeling remains low. Myanmar has retained a system of import and export licensing, thus adding to the documentary requirements.

The establishment of an NSW based on the World Bank model is being driven more by the planned ASEAN Single Window rather than compliance with the TFA. Myanmar Customs, the Ministry of Commerce, port authorities, and chambers of commerce have implemented their e-systems but these are mainly "island based" with limited or no data exchange between them. Network services are available via a virtual private network (VPN). Internet penetration is high, but broadband connectivity is limited and expensive.

Myanmar has no published trade facilitation program for setting out policies and strategies to enhance trade facilitation, although the National Trade Facilitation Action Plan has been drafted by the National Committee for the Trade Facilitation's Secretariat.

Nepal

Trade facilitation in Nepal has in recent years largely been driven by six policy documents. The strategy of the Trade Policy 2015, drawn up by the Ministry of Commerce and Supplies, is to "reduce transaction costs through trade facilitation and institutional strengthening."[15] This was followed by the Nepal Trade Integration Strategy 2016, which is more oriented toward improving the competitiveness of exports. Its proposed reforms include complying with the RKC and the TFA and setting up post-clearance audits, AEO programs, and an NSW. The 14th National Development Plan 2017–2019 has a policy action to address the significant time and costs associated with international trade by simplifying trade procedures and removing NTBs. This was taken forward in the 15th plan 2019/20–2023/24 which re-emphasized the need to reduce internal and external trade costs. The Customs Reform and Modernization Strategic Action Plans 2017–2021 and 2021–2025 also dealt with trade facilitation

Nepal acceded to the RKC in February 2017. A gap analysis by the World Bank identified 29 areas in customs legislation as non-compliant with the RKC. In parallel, Nepal signed the TFA in January 2017. A similar analysis identified similar legislative problems that needed to be resolved to achieve full compliance. A new customs act tabled in Parliament for approval contains provisions that are compliant with the provisions of the RKC convention and the agreement, thus addressing the issues mentioned above.

---

[15] Ministry of Commerce and Supplies. 2015. *Trade Policy*. Kathmandu.

Different institutions are responsible for various aspects of trade facilitation. The Ministry of Industry, Commerce and Supplies is the nodal agency tasked with progressing and coordinating trade and WTO matters. It is responsible for notifying the WTO of progress in the TFA's implementation. The ministry set up the National Committee on Trade Facilitation, which is chaired by a ministry secretary; the committee has 20 members from government agencies and trade-related organizations and is nominally responsible for harmonizing trade facilitation initiatives. Other parties that deal with trade facilitation are under the ministry's jurisdiction, including the Intermodal Transport Development Board, which oversees ICDs; the Transit and Warehousing Company, which oversees transit traffic through Kolkata and Haldia ports; and the Bureau of Standards and Metrology, which is responsible for technical regulations and compliance with trading standards. Other parties in trade facilitation include the Ministry of Urban Development, responsible for establishing integrated check posts (ICPs); and the Ministry of Agriculture and Livestock Development, responsible for sanitary and phytosanitary measures. The Department of Customs comes under the Ministry of Finance and has 36 main land customs offices, including those at the ICDs and ICPs.

Current Situation

The modernization of customs services has largely focused on automation. ASYCUDA was launched in 1996 with ADB funding, but its implementation has been beset by technical problems arising from a combination of insufficient local IT capacity, lack of an efficient wide area network, poor staff acceptance, and limited support from the United Nations Conference on Trade and Development. In 2017 the system was upgraded to ASYCUDA World, a web-based application and hence more easily accessed by customs brokers. Improvements have been made in networking such that the systems now have online links to all the customs borders and greater staff acceptance. Brokers can make their declarations online and the system's risk-based selectivity module determines whether shipments need to be examined or not.

Limited progress has been made in rationalizing documentation. Imports other than from India still require a minimum of eight documents plus the declaration—and in addition supplementary documents may be needed by other agencies. Imports from India require marginally fewer documents. Export shipments need a minimum of four documents for customs, plus additional documentation if needed for other agencies (depending on the product). Launched in 2021, the NSW in which 27 different government agencies have so far been integrated allows traders to make one submission of all the required documents for imports through a single point of entry.

A trade portal was established in 2016 with World Bank assistance. It is designed to provide the business community with secure and personalized single-entry point-to-trade information, including regulatory requirements, procedures, and fees. It also has a searchable library of all available documents and material on trade in Nepal. The portal is linked to 14 ministries, 9 departments, including customs, and 4 private sector representatives. The site is also particularly used for public sector tendering purposes.

Significant emphasis has been attached to upgrading border infrastructure. A problem was that the main border crossings were located within border towns, which had significant flows of cross-border and domestic freight movements, as well as large volumes of passenger traffic. The result was major urban congestion, as well as within the border control zone. India has funded the construction of ICPs at Birgunj in 2018 and Biratnagar in 2020. These facilities are located outside towns, with the old border crossing now being used for passenger traffic. The further building of ICPs has been delayed, principally because of land acquisition and access problems on the Indian side. An ICP is planned at Bhairahawa and one is being built at Nepalgunj.

Nepal now has ICDs or land ports at all the main borders. The Sirsiya ICD at the Birgunj border is next to the new ICP and is the country's only rail-connected ICD, handling block trains to and from Kolkata and Visakhapatnam ports. The new ICP at Biratnagar will replace the ICD. Karkarbitta and Bhairahawa have ICDs; these are operated by private companies with customs approval.

A gap analysis of Nepal's implementation of the WTO TFA in January 2017 by the World Bank highlighted that out of the 36 measures the legislation was only aligned in 2 cases, mainly aligned in 11, partially aligned in 16, and not aligned in 7. By 2021, 3 measures were Category A, 16 Category B, and 16 Category C. There was a significant improvement from 2018 to 2021, with 10 articles being moved from Category C to B and 1 from Category B to A. Nepal has notified the WTO that it needs assistance and support for capacity building for implementing the following Category C measures: 1.2, 1.3, 2.1,4, 5.1,5.3, 7.4, 7.7, 7.8, 8, 9, 10.1, 10.3,10.4, and 12. Table A.1.5 shows the implementation status. Despite the progress achieved, Nepal's implementation of the TFA is only 2.1%, according to the WTO.

Table A.1.5: Implementation Status of the Trade Facilitation Agreement in Nepal

Article	Description	Status
1.1	Publication	B: Rules and procedures of border agencies are published in the Nepal Gazette, but administrative rules are not, though they are available on agency websites.
1.2	Information available through the internet	C: Trade portal established with 14 Ministries, 9 departments, including customs, and 4 private sector representatives, but not user-friendly in current form.
1.3	Enquiry points	C: Enquiry points established, but lack definition.
2.1	Opportunity for comment and information	C: Consultation takes place between government agencies and the private sector.
2.2	Consultation	B: National Trade Facilitation Committee was formed, but not functioning systemically to enhance trade facilitation.
3	Advanced rulings	B: Advanced rulings on classification and origin came into effect in February 2020.
4	Procedures for appeal	C: Legal problems in its implementation.
5.1	Notification of advanced controls or inspections	C: Lack of advanced controls for import alert and early warning systems for sanitary and phytosanitary matters.
5.2	Detention	B: System in place, but no provision to notify importer if goods are detained.
5.3	Test procedures	C: Well-equipped central laboratory at the Department of Customs with second testing done as and when required, this issue is included in the new customs act before parliament.
6.1	Fees and charges	B: System in place, though no provision for delayed effective dating.
6.2	Discipline on fees and charges	B: Fees published, although the basis of the fee structure is not included.
6.3	Penalty discipline	B: System in place, but legal provisions are ambiguous and do not address voluntary disclosures.
7.1	Pre-arrival processing	B: Declaration can be submitted before the arrival of goods. Provision for pre-arrival processing is included in the new customs act before parliament.
7.2	Electronic payment	B: No provision in ASYCUDA for online electronic payments via central bank or Rasta Bank. Payments need to be made separately and receipt submitted for clearance.

continued on next page

Table A.1.5 continued

Article	Description	Status
7.3	Separation of release from the final determination	B: A system in place to pay a deposit for fees and duties before final determination, but the existing customs act needs adjusting to allow the release of goods before determination.
7.4	Risk management	C: Risk management system in place with channeling, but the system needs revalidation methodology with random checking of compliance to ensure it remains current.
7.5	Post clearance audit	B: Customs has a post-audit office and can undertake checks, but the system is not integrated with the risk management module.
7.6	Average release times	B: Three time-release studies were conducted and recommendations are being implemented.
7.7	Authorized economic operator (AEO)	C: Provisions for AEOs included in the new customs act before parliament.
7.8	Expedited shipments	C: System is in place but lacks guidelines on its application.
7.9	Perishable goods	B: Perishables are generally given priority, but the legislation does not allow for overtime clearances and citing of reasons for delays.
8	Border agency cooperation	C: Customs Trade Facilitation Committee holds meetings with other border agencies and stakeholders centrally and at field offices.
9	Import under customs control	C: Customs act has been amended to allow inland transit of imported goods to the ICD constructed at Chobhar.
10.1	Formalities and documentation requirements	C: Customs Reform and Modernization Plan 2021–2025 and the draft new customs act are the main policy documents guiding the review of formalities and document requirements.
10.2	Acceptance of copies	B: The system allows acceptance of copies for online declarations, but not all brokers declare online so originals have to be submitted on lodgment.
10.3	Use of international standards	C: The new customs act before parliament has provisions aligned with the Revised Kyoto Convention and Trade Facilitation Agreement making it partially compliant with international standards.
10.4	Single window	A: Contractor appointed by World Bank to establish an NSW in August 2019; with 21 agencies expected to participate. NSW opened in 2021 so now considered A.
10.5	Pre-shipment inspection	A: System in place.
10.6	Use of customs brokers	A: Importers and exporters use customs brokers.
10.7	Common border procedures	B: ASYCUDA provides standardization of procedures, but practices can vary between borders due to the lack of formal operating standards.
10.8	Rejected goods	B: No transparent procedures for the return of goods, although permitted by legislation.
10.9	Temporary admission	B: Legal provision exists and is being practiced.
11	Freedom of transit	C: Provisions and customs transit rules exist, but require legislation to be compliant with the Trade Facilitation Agreement.
12	Customs cooperation	B: Nepal participates in customs cooperation meetings of SAARC and SASEC. A Customs Mutual Assistance Agreement has been signed with the People's Republic of China.
23	National Committee on Trade Facilitation	A: National Trade Facilitation Committee was formed in 2012, but lacks a legal mandate to implement changes.

A = full implementation, B = part implementation, C = signifying that implementation will need external assistance

Sources: Asian Development Bank. 2019. *Borders without Barriers: Facilitating Trade in SASEC Countries*; Department of Customs; 24 February 2021 notification to the World Trade Organization; Asian Development Bank.

The Department of Customs has undertaken measures to address the constraints caused by COVID-19. To ensure the smooth functioning of customs offices under the pandemic safety protocols, they formed the quick response team under the deputy director-general of the Department of Customs with the mandate of resolving deadlocks in the clearance of essential goods and ensuring the unhindered continuation of supply chains. A guideline was instituted during the pandemic that allowed for the deferred submission of the documentation required for customs clearance and the establishment of a dedicated unit for expediting the clearance of essential goods.

Outstanding Concerns

Excessive documentation requirements remain a constraint to enhancing Nepal's trade facilitation situation. The numerous government agencies involved in trade facilitation, each with their own legislative responsibilities, may be a factor in the continuing problem of excessive documentation. Time-release studies show import shipments via Kolkata can sometimes require over 20 original documents and almost 50 copies to complete over 20 procedures. The problem of delays in border clearance is often not the actual processing, but more commonly the time taken to accumulate the required documents for lodgment. Time-release studies suggest that 70%-85% of border transit time is spent collating documents. With the NSW coming on stream, border transit times should theoretically be significantly reduced.

Significant progress has been made in upgrading and modernizing border infrastructure in recent years—notably the construction and commissioning of ICPs at Birgunj and Biratnagar. These facilities are based on a standard design developed by a subsidiary of Indian Railways, with almost no operational input at the time from the Department of Customs. Indications are the final product has not resulted in significantly enhanced processing performance, and in some cases has created additional operational problems. The newly planned ICPs are now being designed with inputs from the Department of Customs on their layout, and these facilities should therefore be more calibrated to the specific needs of customs operations at that location.

Nepal's ICDs are all located adjacent to border crossings. They would probably be called land ports by other BIMSTEC countries—the exception being Sirsiya, which handles container trains from Kolkata and Visakhapatnam. While some of these lack size and the presence of all border agencies, improvements may be difficult in the short- to medium-term if they are cited to be replaced with an ICP. A potential issue is the ICDs are mainly operated by private operators under the Ministry of Industry, Commerce and Supplies, whereas the ICPs are under the Ministry of Urban Development. The ICPs are so large that they supersede the need for an ICD or land port at that crossing. The recently completed ICD at Chobhar, Kathmandu will allow goods to be transited directly from the border to the primary source of import demand, and the existing customs act has been amended to provide the legal basis for inland transit.

Nepal faces sanitary and phytosanitary barriers and trading standards barriers due to capacity constraints. It lacks accredited laboratories, which affects import and export movements. In the absence of mutual recognition agreements, this means that certain products have to be retested in the country of destination. Reforms are needed to rationalize the diverse requirements of the various government agencies to help simplify overall procedures.

The terms of the National Trade and Transport Facilitation Committee are to:

- review and advise on regulatory reform to facilitate domestic and international trade;
- monitor and coordinate activities for trade, transport, and transit facilitation;
- build capacity or facilitate training and skills development of public and private sector institutions involved in trade facilitation;
- identify best practices and implement these in a country context;
- suggest measures to simplify and harmonize practices, consistent with the objectives of facilitating trade;
- improve coordination among and increase dialogue among trade and transport agencies;
- provide policy feedback for advancing the concept of cooperation in trade, transport, and transit facilitation at the subregional and regional levels;
- promote training and research in international trade, transit, and transport and upgrade stakeholder knowledge on international practices;
- promote the adoption of standard trade and transport terminology, particularly the use of International Chamber of Commerce Terms; and
- mobilize trade-related technical assistance and aid for trade and transport facilitation.

The extensive scope of this remit shows trade facilitation in Nepal needs further reform and modernization if it is to achieve world standards. The remit of the national trade and transport facilitation committees in other BIMSTEC countries tends to be more focused than Nepal's, and it is questionable whether the committee can achieve all these diverse goals without prioritizing some measures.

Sri Lanka

Sri Lanka is a signatory to several international agreements and conventions that affect trade facilitation. As a WCO member, Sri Lanka signed the RKC that came into force in Sri Lanka in February 2006. The country is also a signatory to the Sanitary and Phytosanitary Agreement, the Technical Barriers to Trade Agreement, and the Valuation Agreement. Sri Lanka ratified the WTO TFA in May 2016, which came into force in February 2017. Sri Lanka has also signed bilateral and regional free trade agreements that include articles for simplifying clearance procedures, harmonization of standards, MRAs, and transit aspects. These are predominantly recommendations rather than being mandatory.

Three main parties are involved in advancing trade facilitation: Sri Lanka Customs, the Department of Commerce, and the Sri Lanka Ports Authority. The remit of Sri Lanka Customs is to "enforce revenue and social protection laws of the state while facilitating trade with the objective of contributing to the national effort and in due recognition thereof."[16] The Department of Commerce is responsible for trade policies and is more concerned with tariff aspects and the issuing of certificates-of-origin. However, the department is also the WTO's focal point and therefore responsible for the TFA implementation. Overall, there are an estimated 34 government agencies involved in issuing permits and publishing regulations for trade facilitation matters.

---

[16] Sri Lanka Customs. *Mission Statement.* https://www.customs.gov.lk/about-us/overview/.

Current Situation

Sri Lanka's trade facilitation performance has, going by international surveys, been slipping in recent years. In the World Bank's Trading Across Borders indicator, Sri Lanka fell to 99th rank out of 190 countries in the 2020 survey from 96th in the previous year. In the World Economic Forum's 2016 Global Enabling Trade Report, Sri Lanka fell to 103rd out of 134 economies from 96th in 2014. In the World Bank's 2018 Logistics Performance Index, Sri Lanka ranked 94th. Clearly, Sri Lanka has trade facilitation challenges to be addressed.

Colombo is a major container hub for the BIMSTEC region (along with ports in the Straits of Malacca). Most container shipments handled in Colombo port are transit containers, which largely either originate in or are destined for BIMSTEC countries, and this underlines the importance of resolving the country's trade facilitation challenges, which potentially can have regional implications. Changes were recently introduced to promote less-than-containerload operators to use facilities in Colombo to collate or redistribute consolidation traffic to or from other BIMSTEC countries and to use Sri Lanka as a center for their GVC activities.

Sri Lanka Customs is the chief agency covering trade facilitation. It administers and implements the main legislation governing customs procedures under the Customs Ordinance of 1988, and it sets the rules, regulations, and procedures governing the country's export and import processes. This legislation has undergone several amendments—the most recent being the Customs (Amendment) Act No. 2 of 2003 for implementing the WTO Valuation Agreement. Sri Lanka Customs has drafted required amendments to the Customs Ordinance to make the legal provisions for implementing the Trade Facilitation Agreement. These were submitted to the Ministry of Finance in the second quarter of 2019. Many of the Category C Trade Facilitation Agreement classifications relate to the need to update customs legislation.

The main emphasis on customs modernization is through increased automation. Although the Electronic Data Interchange was introduced in 2008, the most important advance was introducing ASYCUDA World in 2012. The risk-based automated cargo selectivity mechanism has paved the way to recognize compliant traders under the two-fold scheme, either green channel or fast track. This has recently been reviewed and there are now 40 companies enjoying green channel and 177 using fast track facilities.

A customs single window was launched in 2016 allowing customs to issue clearances online. In recognition of the importance of container operations, container examination and release procedures have been streamlined and some port facilitation measures relating to less-than-containerload traffic improved. Changes have also been made in port gate procedures to reduce traffic queuing.

A National Trade Facilitation Committee was set up in 2014 to oversee the planning and implementation of reforms. It was formalized in 2016 in preparation for the ratification of the TFA. The committee's functions are to identify bottlenecks and inefficiencies in trade procedures, make recommendations to guide reform, and coordinate interagency activities. It is co-chaired by the director generals of Sri Lanka Customs and the Department of Commerce, with committee representation being the heads of 16 government agencies and seven members representing the private sector. With such a large number of participants, concerns have been raised about the level of commitment by some parties to achieving the committee's overall goals.

In 2018, the Department of Commerce and the National Trade Facilitation Committee established a trade information portal, with funding from the World Bank and the Government of Australia. The portal is a dedicated platform for trade-related regulatory information on imports and exports identifying commodities subject to regulatory controls and has information on the ministries involved in regulating import/export processes and on related laws and regulations.

The government's Vision 2025 strategy was drawn up to improve trade facilitation. It sets out policies to improve trade logistics and establish efficient and transparent customs procedures, among other things.[17] The 2017 National Trade Policy highlights the Vision 2025 pillar of expanding market access and enhancing trade facilitation, and the need to implement the following as soon as possible:

- Harmonization and simplification of procedures;
- More transparent, predictable, and accessible laws, rules, and regulations;
- Publishing trade facilitation processing documents on a single platform;
- Providing enquiry points;
- Establishing an NSW;
- Modern customs methodologies to ensure the speedy release of goods;
- Completing MRAs; and
- Stakeholder consultation.

Table A.1.6 estimates compliance levels with the TFA, including their reported implementation categories. Sri Lanka's current implementation level is 31.5%, though no notifications to the WTO have been made since 2018 to indicate changes in the status of the categories.

Table A.1.6: Implementation Status of the Trade Facilitation Agreement in Sri Lanka

Article	Description	Status
1.1	Publication	C: Systems in place, but tends to not publish changes in advance.
1.2	Information available through the internet	C: Trade portal, completed in 2018, provides regulatory information on imports and exports. Need for constant updating.
1.3	Enquiry points	C: System in place, but staff capacity can be an issue. Indications were that World Bank assistance might be available.
1.4	Notification	C: System in place through the trade portal.
2.1	Opportunity for comment and information	C: Mechanisms are in place through the National Trade Facilitation Committee among others, but tend to be in retrospect rather than in advance.
2.2	Consultation	C: The consultation process exists, but its effectiveness may be a concern.
3	Advanced rulings	C: System in place, but not widely used or legally binding,
4	Procedures for appeal	A: System in place, but it may not be compliant with TFA requirements due to the lack of an appellant body.
5.1	Notification of advanced controls or inspections	C: Requires design and support of a notification system.
5.2	Detention	A: Compliant with a system in place.

continued on next page

[17]   These were the policies of the previous government and it is appreciated they could potentially be changed by the new government, which came to power in August 2020.

Table A.1.6 continued

Article	Description	Status
5.3	Test procedures	C: Lack of facilities, equipment, and expertise, as well as automation of results.
6.1	Fees and charges	C: Fees and charges published.
6.2	Discipline on fees and charges	C: Basis of fees and charges unclear.
6.3	Penalty discipline	A: Compliant with a system in place.
7.1	Pre-arrival processing	B: System in place, but only for perishable goods and certain items.
7.2	Electronic payment	A: Compliant with e-payments.
7.3	Separation of release from the final determination	C: No compliant system in place.
7.4	Risk management	C: System in place using ASYCUDA module and channeling, but the percentage of orange and red channels remains high.
7.5	Post clearance audit	C: System-based audit program in customs with donor assistance from ADB.
7.6	Average release times	C: Some time-release studies have been conducted, but no formal structure for regular studies.
7.7	Authorized economic operator	C: System in place, but only with limited application to the private sector.
7.8	Expedited shipments	A: Special procedures exist.
7.9	Perishable goods	C: The system exists, but suffers from poor operational coordination between agencies.
8	Border agency cooperation	C: Cooperation at a high level, such as the National Trade Facilitation Committee, but less so at an operational level.
9	Import under customs control	A: Compliant with a system in place.
10.1	Formalities and documentation requirements	C: Need for further reviews on how to streamline procedures.
10.2	Acceptance of copies	C: Requires legal changes.
10.3	Use of international standards	C: Need for capacity building on international standards and best practices.
10.4	Single window	C: NSW Project Implementation Unit has been established under the guidance of the Ministry of Finance. In consultation with the high-level Steering Committee, the Project Implementation Committee has developed a way forward for the initiation, implementation, and operationalization of the NSW.
10.5	Pre-shipment inspection	B: System in place, but not widely used.
10.6	Use of customs brokers	A: Importers and exporters use customs house agents.
10.7	Common border procedures	A: Compliant with a system in place
10.8	Rejected goods	A: Compliant with a system in place.
10.9	Temporary admission	A: Compliant with a system in place.
11	Freedom of transit	A: Compliant with a system in place.
12	Customs cooperation	C: Cooperation in the form of WCO, SAARC, and SASEC meetings, rather than bilaterally.
23	National Committee on Trade Facilitation	A: Established in 2014; formalized in 2016.

A = full implementation, B = part implementation, C = signifying that implementation will need external assistance.

Sources: Asian Development Bank. 2019. *Borders without Barriers: Facilitating Trade in SASEC Countries*. Manila; Asian Development Bank.

Outstanding Concerns

Sri Lanka's large number of TFA Category C ratings is a cause for concern. Many of these low ratings relate to the lack of supporting legislation that is delaying the implementation of the new customs ordinance compatible with the agreement and the latest best practices in customs processes and procedures. This new legislation, when passed, should enable a significant number of Category C measures to be implemented and then re-rated to Category A.

Significant progress has been in automating customs activities, but the benefits have yet to be fully realized. Traders and their agents file their declarations electronically, but most of the supporting documentation still has to be presented physically. In addition, during the various stages of clearance, manual signatures are still required. The result is that both manual and automated systems are working in parallel, negating many of the benefits of automation. However, the use of digital signatures for processing of declarations ensures the speedy clearance and forwarding of shipments that have such validation of authenticity and integrity of the digital documentation within the legitimate environment. Customs introduced digital signatures to trade highlighting its benefits, and the process of clearing import and export consignments using only the digital signature is now taking place.

The containers requiring regulatory controls are as high as 40% of all imports. In the current context, Sri Lanka Customs has no choice but to refer all such containers to examination yards for drawing samples by other regulatory agencies that have not been able to implement risk management within their procedures. Accordingly, it has become necessary to refer a higher number of consignments for examination merely to meet regulatory requirements. The containers selected as high-risk cargo are between 10-12%, while another 5% of containers are classified as medium risk thereby meeting the intrusive examination requirements of customs. Sri Lanka Customs established a National Import Valuation Database Unit in 2021 as a risk management tool for customs valuation to assist officers by providing values on imported goods.

Significant gaps in sanitary and phytosanitary activities emanate from the lack of updated legislation for international best practices, duplication and overlapping functions, and shortages of laboratories, test equipment, and trained personnel. Similarly, the Standards Institute needs strengthening, as there is a shortage of laboratories and equipment and no MRA with other countries. In addition, not all the sanitary, phytosanitary, and trading standards organizations have the same level of IT usage as customs and can issue certificates and clearances online. This will become an increasing constraint as Sri Lanka develops its NSW. The National Trade Facilitation Committee is discussing with the World Bank and ADB for donor assistance for the development of standards of procedure with regard to the test procedures at all the government agencies that have laboratory facilities and for the upgrading of the customs laboratory to the standard necessary to achieve laboratory accreditation.

Port facilitation is particularly important in Sri Lanka given Colombo's role as a hub port with performance bring critical not only for Sri Lanka's international trade but also for other BIMSTEC countries, albeit to varying degrees. Colombo lacks a PCS and the recent port masterplan was drawn up with assistance from ADB highlighted this deficiency[18]. If Colombo is to retain its role as a hub port and

---

[18] Asian Development Bank. 2020. *Democratic Socialist Republic of Sri Lanka: National Port Master Plan.* Manila. https://www.adb. org/projects/50184-001/main.

share of Indian transshipments, it must have the advanced tools to ensure that its transit performance is further improved.

The economic crisis in 2022 represents a severe trade facilitation setback in the short- to medium-term. Imports in particular would be expected to fall sharply due to the lack of finance to purchase goods from overseas. In addition, exports will also be impacted by the shortages of fuel and in some cases materials. Unfortunately, the main container lines are already bypassing Colombo port using their other hubs, particularly in the Straits of Malacca, to service Sri Lanka's residual import/export trade, with the Indian traffic now being rerouted direct from these hub ports. The temporary loss of this major transshipment flow and lower national import and export shipments will appreciably reduce overall trade facilitation activity. Measures such as approval of the new customs act and the development of the PCS are likely to stall until the situation is stabilized and international loan assistance is finalized. The problem of debt financing may also potentially limit further loans from the IFIs, including any for trade facilitation infrastructure projects, but should not necessarily affect technical assistance provided by these external organizations.

Thailand

Thailand, as a WCO member, is a signatory to the RKC, the Convention Establishing a Customs Co-operation Council, and the Customs Convention on Temporary Admission (Istanbul Convention). Thailand became the 20th WTO member to accede to the TFA when it submitted its instrument of acceptance ratifying the agreement in 2017.

Three main parties are responsible for trade facilitation. The first is the Ministry of Finance, which has four departments engaged in trade matters: customs, excise, revenue, and the Tobacco Authority. The second is the Ministry of Commerce, which has departments engaged in foreign and domestic trade, external and intellectual property, and business development. The third is the Ministry of Agriculture and Cooperatives, which has departments engaged in livestock development, fisheries, and agriculture. The National Bureau of Agricultural Commodity and Food Standards is also part of this ministry. The Ministry of Finance, through Royal Thai Customs, is the apex body for most trade facilitation matters. The Ministry of Commerce is more oriented toward trade and tariff matters, and the Ministry of Agriculture and Cooperatives is responsible for sanitary and phytosanitary.

Current Situation

The mission of Royal Thai Customs is to facilitate trade and promote a national logistics system, advance the national economy through customs-related measures and international trade information, protect and secure society based on customs control systems, and collect revenue in a fair, transparent, and efficient manner. Thailand is the only BIMSTEC country whose customs have trade facilitation as its primary mission, and also includes logistics in its remit. Designated strategies to achieve this mission are to improve:

- Work processes and ICT systems for trade facilitation;
- Measures and trade information to promote border trade and global trade connectivity;
- Efficient and integrated customs controls;
- Efficient revenue collection efficiency based on good governance principles; and
- Human resources capacity and organizational management.

Royal Thai Customs has implemented a new form of computer automation system called e-Customs. Traders must register to use the system and, when that is done, they receive a digital certificate. This is used to affirm the identity of the sender of electronic documents and is fundamental for all organizations in Thailand with online activities, including import and export registration. The system provides a one-stop service for all stakeholders in international trade. Procedures such as issuing licenses, paying duties and taxes, cargo control, and goods declaration processing have been made paperless and can be completed using the central 'e-Customs' system with its e-import, e-export, e-manifest, e-payment, and e-warehouse modules.

Thailand began advancing an NSW back in 2005, with the Cabinet appointing the Royal Thai Customs as the lead agency. The system began initial operations in 2008 and was officially launched in October 2011. Government agencies and business communities agreed to adopt the ebXML standard for the NSW, using digital signatures for the secure exchange of electronic documents. The NSW has over 10,000 subscribers serving 100,000 trading companies. Some 38 authorities, including government and business agencies, are participating in the system, which has been administered by the National Logistics Development Committee since 2017.

The National Trade Repository acts as a trade portal and is the responsibility of the Ministry of Commerce's Department of Trade Negotiations. Other concerned government agencies are obligated to provide the department with information on trade measures and regulations, which are then compiled in the repository. It has three main features: trade in goods, trade in services, and e-commerce. Trade in goods is the most relevant to trade facilitation as it provides updated information on tariff nomenclature, harmonized tariff schedules, rules of origin, national trade and customs laws and regulations, procedures and documentary requirements, administrative and court rulings, best practices in trade facilitation, AEOs, and related organizations linked into the system.

The AEO program of Royal Thai Customs was initiated in 2011. Because participation was initially low, the European Union provided technical assistance to increase its effectiveness. The EU study proposed taking the following measures to increase participation:

- Making the program smoother and low cost;
- Investing in systematic design;
- Implementing and monitoring AEO benefits and incentives;
- Promoting multi-agency cooperation under the customs AEO umbrella;
- Shifting to system-based and audit-based principles and practices;
- Expanding to include other actors eligible for AEO status; and
- Moving toward several AEO MRAs with third countries and regions.

In 2020, Thailand had issued AEO certificates to 385 companies, of which 198 were importers or exporters and 187 were customs brokers. Most undergo post-authorization audits every 3 years. MRAs have been signed with several countries.

Table A.1.7 estimates the compliance levels with the TFA and their reported implementation categories. Thailand has implemented 97.1% of the agreement, though it is noted that Thailand has not updated its notifications with the WTO since 2018.

Table A.1.7: Implementation Status of the Trade Facilitation Agreement in Thailand

Article	Description	Status
1.1	Publication	A: Compliant.
1.2	Information available through the internet	A: Compliant with trade portal established.
1.3	Enquiry points	A: Various enquiry points exist, but no centralized system.
1.4	Notification	A: Compliant in making notifications in advance.
2.1	Opportunity for comment and information	A: Compliant with a system in place.
2.2	Consultation	A: National Trade and Transport Committee in place.
3	Advanced rulings	A: Compliant with a system in place.
4	Procedures for appeal	A/B: Compliant, but 4.4 awaiting implementation.
5.1	Notification of advanced controls or inspections	A: Compliant with a system in place.
5.2	Detention	A: Compliant with a system in place.
5.3	Test procedures	B: Non-compliant as still awaiting full implementation.
6.1	Fees and charges	A: Compliant with a system in place for publishing.
6.2	Discipline on fees and charges	A: Compliant with a system in place.
6.3	Penalty discipline	A/B: Partly compliant, but 6.3.4 not yet implemented.
7.1	Pre-arrival processing	A/B: Partly compliant, but 7.1.1 not yet implemented.
7.2	Electronic payment	A: Compliant with e-banking memorandum of understanding signed in 2019.
7.3	Separation of release from the final determination	A: Compliant with a system in place.
7.4	Risk management	A: Compliant with a system in place.
7.5	Post clearance audit	A: Compliant with a system in place.
7.6	Average release times	A: Compliant with a system in place with results being published.
7.7	Authorized economic operator	A: Compliant with a system in place.
7.8	Expedited shipments	A: Compliant with a system in place.
7.9	Perishable goods	A: Compliant with a system in place.
8	Border agency cooperation	A: Compliant with a system in place.
9	Import under customs control	A: Compliant with a system in place.
10.1	Formalities and documentation requirements	A: Compliant with a system in place.
10.2	Acceptance of copies	A: Compliant with a system in place.
10.3	Use of international standards	A: Compliant with a system in place.
10.4	Single window	A: National single window in operation.
10.5	Pre-shipment inspection	A: Compliant with a system in place.
10.6	Use of customs brokers	A: Customs brokers used.
10.7	Common border procedures	A: Compliant with a system in place.
10.8	Rejected goods	A: Compliant with a system in place.

continued on next page

Table A.1.7 continued

Article	Description	Status
10.9	Temporary admission	A: Compliant with a system in place.
11	Freedom of transit	A/B: Partly compliant but 11.1, 11.8, and 11.9 are not fully implemented.
12	Customs cooperation	A/B Part compliant but 12.2 not fully implemented.
23	National Committee on Trade Facilitation	A: National Committee on Trade Facilitation in place.

A = full implementation, B = part implementation, C = signifying that implementation will need external assistance Sources: World Trade Organization Database. Trade Facilitation Agreement Database. (Accessed 15 October 2020); Asian Development Bank.

Outstanding Concerns

Trade facilitation in Thailand is more advanced than in other BIMSTEC countries. The country's 97.1% TFA implementation demonstrates its success in introducing more advanced methodologies. Even so, the process of reforming and modernizing trade facilitation does not end with 100% compliance as Thailand moves forward to TFA+ and higher rankings in international indexes and surveys. Challenges that the country faces identified in these external surveys relate to relatively low rankings and scores on fees and charges, advanced rulings, transit, information availability, and border and institutional cooperation. The TFA tends to be customs-centric, and it is unlikely that other border agencies, such as those responsible for sanitary, phytosanitary, and trading standards matters, are as advanced, despite their active participation in the NSW.

Much of the emphasis on enhancing trade facilitation in Thailand comes from its membership of ASEAN, where it is competing with countries with even more advanced trade facilitation conditions, such as Singapore and Malaysia. The Royal Thai Customs has a clear development strategy representing its pathway to TFA+, but it is not clear whether other border agencies have complementary strategies, especially as their institutional cooperation performance is not rated highly in international surveys.

Thailand does not as yet have a PCS. A contract was signed in 2019 for establishing a system with Hamburg Port Consulting and a local company. It is anticipated that this system will be eventually linked to e-customs and NSW applications. Reducing port dwell times further will be essential for enhancing the performance of the country's seaports, and this will only be achieved by further improving port and trade facilitation in parallel.

Thailand has its National Transport and Trade Facilitation Committee, but its membership, remit, and strategic goals have not been made public. Trade facilitation is not cited in Thailand's Voluntary National Review on the Implementation of the 2030 Agenda for Sustainable Development or in its 20-year national strategy.

EXTERNAL PERCEPTIONS OF BAY OF BENGAL INITIATIVE FOR MULTI-SECTORAL TECHNICAL AND ECONOMIC COOPERATION (BIMSTEC) TRADE FACILITATION PERFORMANCE

This appendix shows where the BIMSTEC region stands concerning the implementation of various trade facilitation measures. It needs to be stated at the outset that some member states' data has not been updated recently and that certain indexes are based on perceptions rather than factually-based statistics. Even so, international surveys provide an element of benchmarking and represent external views on the status of the implementation of modern trade facilitation in the BIMSTEC region. The initial sections (B1–3) relate more to the narrow interpretation of trade facilitation, focusing on enhancements in customs and border procedures. Sections B4–5 expand the scope toward the "new generation" interpretation of trade facilitation by examining it from a more logistical perspective.

World Trade Organization Trade Facilitation Agreement

The WTO recognizes the need to address trade facilitation from the standpoint of the simplification, modernization, and harmonization of export and import processes. WTO members concluded negotiations in 2013 on a TFA, which came into force in 2017 when two-thirds of members ratified it. The agreement has provisions for "expediting the movement, release, and clearance of goods, including goods in transit, and indicates measures for effective cooperation between customs and other appropriate authorities on trade facilitation and customs compliance.[19]" It also includes provisions for technical assistance and capacity building.

The agreement recognizes that trade facilitation situations differ appreciably among the 153 signatory countries, especially between developed, developing, and least developed economies. Because of this, it has special provisions allowing developing and least developed countries to determine their own rates of implementation and their need for technical assistance or support for capacity building to enable implementation. For these countries, which include all BIMSTEC countries, there are three implementation classifications:

- Category A: Provisions members will implement by the time the agreement comes into force (or in the case of a least-developed country within 1 year after this);
- Category B: Provisions members will implement after a transitional period after the agreement comes into force; and
- Category C: Provisions members will implement on a date after a transitional period of the agreement coming into force, and requires assistance and support for capacity building.

---

[19] World Trade Organization. Trade facilitation Agreement: Introduction. Geneva. https://docs.wto.org/dol2fe/Pages/SS/directdoc. aspx?filename=q:/WT/L/940.pdf&Open=True.

Levels of implementation notified to the WTO by BIMSTEC countries indicate that Thailand and India are both at an advanced stage having no Category Cs. Bangladesh and Sri Lanka, the middle group, have fewer Category As, but with appreciable differences in Category C, with Sri Lanka needing more delayed implementation. Myanmar and Nepal have low levels of implementation and a high demand for assistance, although both are making significant progress in implementing the agreement. Bhutan is not a WTO member, but probably has a similar profile to Nepal. The TFA implementation levels broadly reflect the progress that has been made in establishing automated customs systems in the region, with Thailand and India being the most advanced in this respect. One caveat is that changes in the categorization of each of the measures are based on notifications by each country to the WTO. In some cases, no notification or updates have been submitted since 2018. It should also be noted that complying with the TFA is open to different interpretations, given the agreement's flexible wording—for example, the use of "where practical," "shall endeavor to," and "encouraged to." Thus, indications of compliance under the categories may be considered a best-effort rather than confirming actual implementation.

An issue for BIMSTEC's strategic trade facilitation planning is raising the level of implementation of the TFA in the less advanced countries to that being achieved in Thailand and India. To that end, it is important to identify where technical assistance—be it through regional cooperation mechanisms or international funding institutional support programs—is needed to implement the agreement. Table B.1 breaks down the Category C measures that four BIMSTEC countries have identified as needing technical assistance to be able to implement the agreement. It should be noted that while limited updating on the notifications to the WTO has been provided by Myanmar, Nepal, and Sri Lanka since 2018, it may be that some of these measures have now been addressed, enabling a move to Category A or B. The lack of updating on notifications may also suggest that countries have become less interested in implementing TFA.

Table B.1: Category C Measures Needing Implementation Assistance

Article	Description	Bangladesh 20 Jan 20	Myanmar 18 Feb	Nepal 18 Feb	Sri Lanka 19 Aug
1.1	Publication		X		X
1.2	Information available via the internet		X	X	X
1.3	Enquiry points	X		X	X
1.4	Notification		X		X
2	Opportunity to comment		X	X	X
3	Advanced rulings		X		X
4	Procedures for appeal			X	
5.1	Notification of advanced controls		X	X	X
5.3	Test procedures	X	X	X	X
6.1	General disciplines				X
6.2	Specific disciplines				X
7.1	Pre-arrival processing	X	X		
7.2	Electronic payment		X		
7.3	Separation of release		X		X
7.4	Risk management	X	X	X	X

continued on next page

Table B.1 continued

Article	Description	Bangladesh 20 Jan 20	Myanmar 18 Feb	Nepal 18 Feb	Sri Lanka 19 Aug
7.5	Post-clearance audit	X	X		X
7.6	Average release times		X		X
7.7	Trade facilitation measures for AEOs	X	X	X	X
7.8	Expedited shipments	X	X	X	
7.9	Perishable goods	X	X		X
8.0	Border agency cooperation	X	X	X	X
9.0	Movement of goods			X	
10.1	Formalities/document requirements	X	X	X	X
10.2	Acceptance of copies		X		X
10.3	Use of international standards		X	X	X
10.4	Single window	X	X	X	X
10.7	Common border procedures		X		
10.9	Temporary admission		X		
11	Freedom of transit		X		
11.5	Freedom of transit (continuation)	X			
11.9	Freedom of transit (continuation)	X	X		
11.16	Freedom of transit (continuation)	X	X	X	
12	Customs cooperation		X	X	X

BIMSTEC Bay of Bengal Initiative for Multi-Sectoral Technical and Economic Cooperation, AEO = authorized economic operator.
Source World Trade Organization. Trade Facilitation Agreement Database
Table B.1 also shows the primary need for technical assistance in the four countries is risk management and progressing AEO programs, post-clearance auditing, the single window, testing procedures, and border cooperation.

Organisation for Economic Co-operation and Development Trade Facilitation Indicators

The Organisation for Economic Co-operation and Development (OECD) has a set of trade facilitation indicators to help governments improve their border procedures, reduce trade costs, boost trade flows, and reap greater benefits from international trade. The indicators identify areas for action and enable the potential impact of reforms to be assessed. Estimates based on the indicators provide a basis for governments to prioritize trade facilitation actions and mobilize technical assistance and capacity-building for developing countries in a more targeted manner.

The trade facilitation indicators can also help countries to identify their strengths and weaknesses in trade facilitation by measuring the extent to which they have introduced and implemented trade facilitation measures in absolute terms. The indicators can also be used to benchmark performance through a series of quantitative measures relating to border processing covering the full spectrum of border procedures in 163 countries across income levels, geographical regions, and development stages. They address 11 measures with values from 0 to 2, where 2 is the best performance, and are calculated based on the information from the trade facilitation indicators database. Table B.2 shows the indicators of the BIMSTEC countries and a comparison with Singapore as the best trade facilitation performing country in Southeast Asia.

Table B.2: Organisation for Economic Co-operation and Development Trade Facilitation Indicators for BIMSTEC Countries, 2019

Measure	Bangladesh	Bhutan	India	Myanmar	Nepal	Sri Lanka	Thailand	Singapore
Information availability	1.25	0.47	1.91	0.90	0.67	1.19	1.30	1.80
Involvement trade community	1.14	1.17	1.43	0.75	0.43	1.00	1.71	1.91
Advanced rulings	1.14	0.00	1.30	1.27	0.29	0.86	1.71	2.00
Appeal procedures	1.63	1.13	1.25	1.86	1.22	1.63	1.75	2.00
Fees and charges	1.46	1.10	1.69	1.14	1.00	1.46	1.08	1.88
Documents	0.78	0.56	1.44	0.67	0.63	1.25	1.88	1.92
Automation	0.46	0.00	1.69	0.46	0.30	1.20	1.82	1.88
Procedures	0.70	0.61	1.49	0.85	0.80	1.08	1.74	2.00
Internal border cooperation	0.55	0.40	1.91	1.10	0.50	0.60	0.60	1.85
External border cooperation	0.36	0.18	0.91	0.64	0.46	0.09	0.91	1.50
Governance/ impartiality	1.00	0.88	1.75	1.78	1.43	1.44	1.33	0.91
Average	1.00	0.60	1.50	1.00	0.70	1.10	1.40	1.80

BIMSTEC Bay of Bengal Initiative for Multi-Sectoral Technical and Economic Cooperation.

Source: Organisation for Economic Co-operation and Development. Trade Facilitation Indicators Simulator.

India and Thailand have the highest scores in the BIMSTEC region, as they did in the implementation of the TFA, providing further proof that they have the most advanced trade facilitation environments in the BIMSTEC region. Indeed, their scores are gradually closing in on the best-performing OECD countries. That said, both countries score relatively poorly on external border cooperation. Sri Lanka has a higher scoring on the OECD's trade facilitation indicators than suggested by its TFA implementation ranking. Bangladesh and Myanmar had similar scores, and Nepal and Bhutan had the lowest. It is interesting to note that indicators for automation, documents, and procedures broadly tend to reflect their overall average rankings.

United Nations Global Survey on Trade Facilitation and Paperless Trade

The Global Survey on Trade Facilitation and Paperless Trade is conducted by the five United Nations regional commissions, in collaboration with global and regional partners. The purpose of the survey is to collect data and information on trade facilitation and paperless trade from member economies. It covers not only the implementation of measures included in the Trade Facilitation Agreement but also actions to enable paperless trade (i.e., trade using electronic rather than paper-based data and documentation). The survey covers emerging trade facilitation sector constraints and includes approaches to transit facilitation, such as agreements with neighboring countries and customs authorities to limit the physical inspection of transit goods, the use of risk assessment, support for pre-arrival processing for transit traffic, and cooperation between agencies of countries involved in transit traffic. Transit measures are particularly important for BIMSTEC's landlocked members, Bhutan, and Nepal.

The survey is conducted at least biennially, and the gap between surveys enables progress on implementing trade facilitation measures and paperless trade to be better observed. Each of the survey's trade facilitation articles is scored based on either fully implemented, partially implemented, implemented on a pilot basis, or not implemented. Examining individual trade measures and assessing the scores can provide insights into how countries are performing in the implementation of a particular procedure in the TFA. A benefit of the survey is the data group's indicators measuring transparency, formalities, institutional arrangements, and cooperation, as well as the application of paperless trade, transit facilitation, and inclusiveness in trade facilitation. Figure B.1 shows the weighted implementation scores.

In the 2019 survey, perhaps surprisingly, India (71%) had the highest score, marginally above Thailand (70%). This was mainly due to Thailand's having lower scores on transit and trade facilitation and trade facilitation for small and medium-sized enterprises. Myanmar (55%), Sri Lanka (48%), Bangladesh (47%), Nepal (44%), and Bhutan (36%), all scored lower on trade formalities, similar to those in the OECD indicators. Sri Lanka, which has the third-highest score of BIMSTEC countries in the OECD trade facilitation index, is affected by the absence of a transit facilitation score, as it is an island and the survey does not include third-country traffic transiting through Colombo port. Myanmar's score appears unusually high, compared with earlier surveys, particularly for its paperless trade score.

Figure B.1: Implementation of Trade Facilitation Measures—BIMSTEC and Regional Comparators, 2019

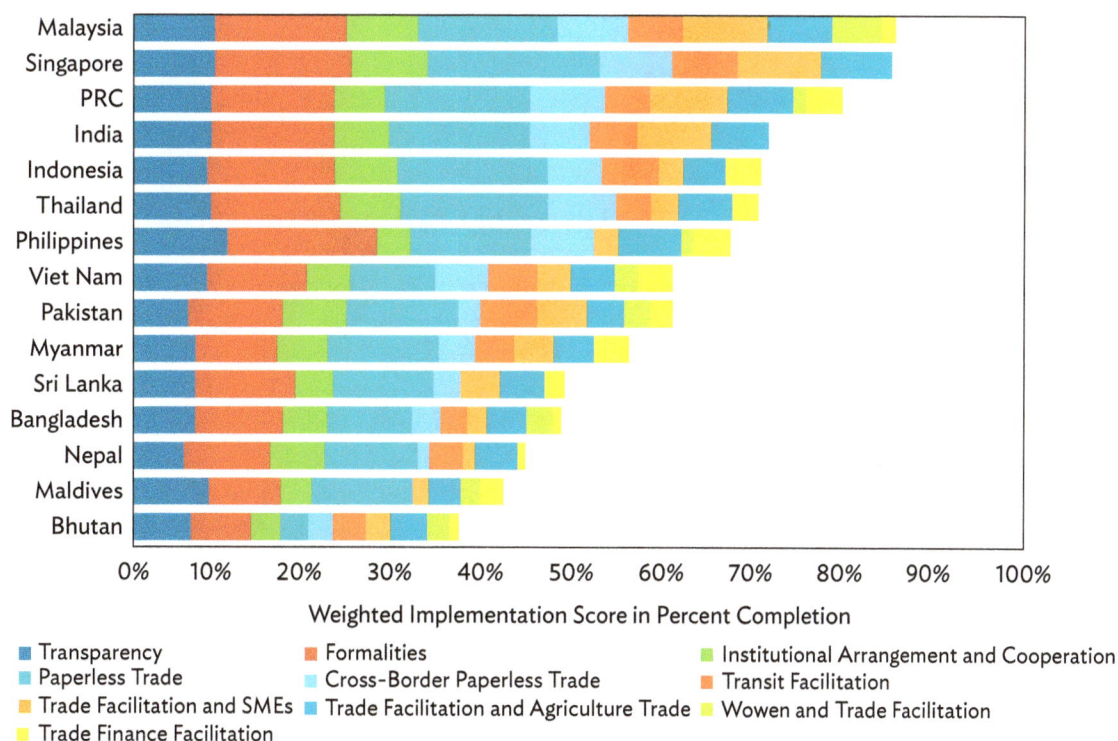

BIMSTEC Bay of Bengal Initiative for Multi-Sectoral Technical and Economic Cooperation, PRC = People's Republic of China, SMEs = small and medium-sized enterprises.

Source: Asian Development Bank. 2019. *Borders without Barriers: Facilitating Trade in SASEC Countries*. Manila.

The United Nations Global Survey on Trade Facilitation and Paperless Trade identified paperless and cross-border paperless scores as the main factors explaining why India and Thailand were ahead of other BIMSTEC countries in terms of trade facilitation. To counter this, the other countries need to establish increased automated processing and this will be a factor in raising their survey scores.

World Bank Logistics Performance Index

The Logistics Performance Index is an interactive benchmarking tool designed to help countries identify the challenges and opportunities from their performance in trade logistics. It can also be used to identify areas where countries need to improve their logistics performance. The index includes all BIMSTEC countries and is based on a survey of freight forwarders and express carriers that provide feedback on the logistics "friendliness" of the countries in the index in which they operate and trade. The index consists of both qualitative and quantitative measures.

2014, 2016, and 2108 Logistic Performance Indexes cover 160 countries; earlier years covered slightly fewer countries. The latest index was published in 2018. Countries are scored on key dimensions to benchmark performance and produce an overall score. The index allows benchmarking comparisons with the world, a region, or an income group, using indicators and an overall score. The six indicators are:

- Customs: the efficiency of the customs clearance processes;
- Infrastructure: the quality of trade and transport-related infrastructure;
- International shipments: the ease of arranging competitively priced shipments;
- Quality of logistics services: the competence and quality of logistics services;
- Tracking and tracing: the ability to track and trace consignments; and
- Timeliness: the frequency with which shipments reach consignees within a scheduled time.

The first two indicators measure the "narrow" definition of trade facilitation. The third measure is a "broad" definition since it relates principally to trade costs. The other three are logistics-oriented toward the "new generation" approach. Table B.3 shows the ranking and score of BIMSTEC countries (scoring is 1–5 score, with 5 being the best). This table to a certain extent replicates the trends evident in the TFA and OECD indicators discussed earlier, showing that Thailand has the most advanced trade facilitation followed by India, and the other BIMSTEC countries coming in significantly behind these two. In this index, Sri Lanka ranks higher than Bangladesh, with Nepal, Myanmar, and Bhutan following.

Table B.3: World Bank Logistics Performance Index Rankings and Scores for BIMSTEC Countries, 2018

Country	Ranking	Score
Bangladesh	100	2.53
Bhutan	149	2.17
India	44	3.18
Myanmar	137	2.30
Nepal	114	2.51
Sri Lanka	94	2.60
Thailand	32	3.41

BIMSTEC Bay of Bengal Initiative for Multi-Sectoral Technical and Economic Cooperation.

World Bank. Logistics Performance Index. https://lpi.worldbank.org/international/global (accessed 9 August 2018).

Table B.4 shows the scoring of each of the measures. Whatever definition of trade facilitation is adopted, the overall pattern remains broadly the same, with Thailand topping the index, followed by India, Sri Lanka, Bangladesh, Nepal, Myanmar, and Bhutan. The scores of Bhutan and Myanmar are particularly low on infrastructure.

Table B.4: World Bank Logistics Performance Index Component Scores for BIMSTEC Countries, 2018

Measure	Bangladesh	Bhutan	India	Myanmar	Nepal	Sri Lanka	Thailand
Customs	2.30	2.14	2.96	2.17	2.29	2.56	3.14
Infrastructure	2.39	1.91	2.91	1.99	2.19	2.49	3.14
International shipments	2.52	1.80	3.21	2.20	2.36	2.51	3.46
Logistics services	2.48	2.35	3.13	2.28	2.46	2.42	3.41
Tracking & tracing	2.79	2.35	3.32	2.20	2.65	2.79	3.47
Timeliness	2.92	2.49	3.58	2.91	3.10	2.79	3.81

BIMSTEC Bay of Bengal Initiative for Multi-Sectoral Technical and Economic Cooperation.
World Bank. Logistics Performance Index. https://lpi.worldbank.org/international/global (accessed 9 August 2018).

Figure B.2 shows the scores of BIMSTEC countries compared with those of other countries in Asia. Singapore and Malaysia are the region's leaders, well ahead of Thailand. Except for Thailand, the other BIMSTEC countries score relatively poorly. Countries involved in global value chains tend to achieve higher rankings, demonstrating the importance of moving toward the "new generation" definition.

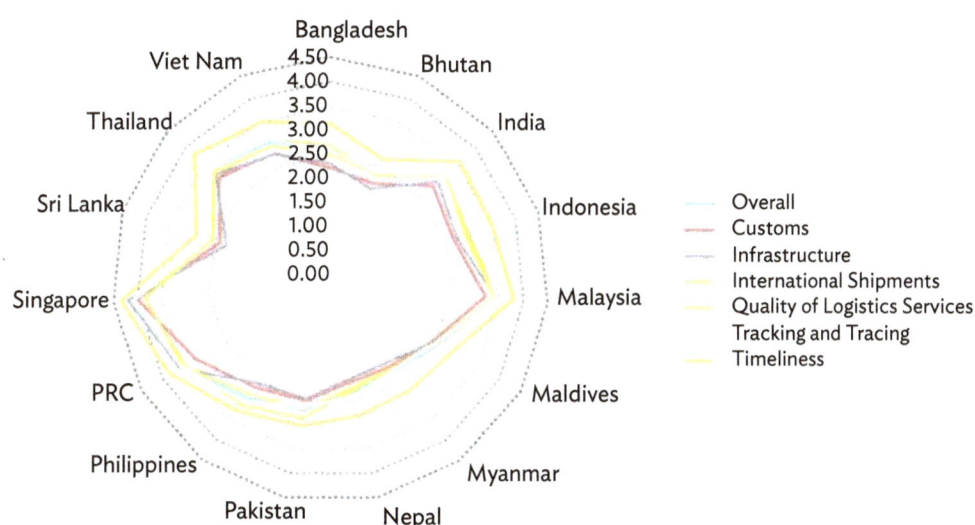

Figure B.2: Average World Bank Logistics Performance Index Scores for BIMSTEC Countries and Other Countries in Asia, 2018

BIMSTEC Bay of Bengal Initiative for Multi-Sectoral Technical and Economic Cooperation, PRC = People's Republic of China, LPI = Logistics Performance Index, SASEC = South Asia Subregional Economic Cooperation.
Source: World Bank. Logistics Performance Index. https://lpi.worldbank.org/international/global (accessed 9 August 2018).

World Bank Doing Business Survey

The World Bank's Doing Business Surveys were started in 2003 to provide objective measures of business regulations and the protection of property rights. It covers 12 indicator areas (or sets) and their enforcement in 190 economies. Indicators include processes for business incorporation, getting a building permit and an electricity connection, transferring property, access to credit, protecting minority investors, paying taxes, engaging in international trade, enforcing contracts, and resolving insolvency. Table B.5 shows the performance of BIMSTEC countries in the 2020 survey.

Table B.5: World Bank Doing Business BIMSTEC Countries Rankings and Scores, 2020

Country	Ranking	Score
Bangladesh	168	45.0
Bhutan	89	66.0
India	62	71.0
Myanmar	165	46.8
Nepal	94	63.2
Sri Lanka	99	61.8
Thailand	21	80.1

BIMSTEC Bay of Bengal Initiative for Multi-Sectoral Technical and Economic Cooperation
World Bank. Doing Business 2004–2020. https://archive.doingbusiness.org/en/doingbusiness (accessed 10 June 2021).

Thailand followed by India is the easiest country in which to do business based on a combination of all the survey indicators. While the results for indicators covering trade facilitation for these countries are the same as earlier survey findings, Bhutan and Nepal scored much better in the 2020 survey than earlier ones. This can be partially explained by their smaller economies, and their simpler rules and regulations. A more precise measure for trade facilitation is the survey's trading across borders indicator. This measures the time and cost associated with exporting and importing goods across three sets of procedures: documentary compliance, border compliance, and domestic transport (Table B.6).

Table B.6: World Bank Doing Business Trading across Border Rankings for BIMSTEC Countries, 2020

	Ranking
Bangladesh	176
Bhutan	30
India	68
Myanmar	168
Nepal	60
Sri Lanka	96
Thailand	62

BIMSTEC Bay of Bengal Initiative for Multi-Sectoral Technical and Economic Cooperation
Source: World Bank. Doing Business Survey 2020.

Table B.6 shows Bhutan and Nepal have the highest rankings. This indicator is particularly oriented toward "compliance" and tends to favor countries with greater amounts of regular cross-border trade with neighbors that often have simpler processes. Larger countries with more global trade inevitably have higher compliance risks. Further analysis of the data based on the broad view of trade facilitation highlights the time and costs of documentation. Time is measured in hours and cost in US dollars capturing access, preparation, processing, presentation, and submission of documents. Figures B.3 and B.4 show the results compared with other economies in Asia.

Figure B.3 shows the extensive time incurred in Bangladesh and Myanmar in collating import and export documentation and in Myanmar for exports, as well as the significant time incurred in clearing imports and exports in Nepal and to a lesser extent in Sri Lanka. Bhutan scores well, possibly because of its low trading volumes and high dependence on cross-border traffic with India under their specific trade and transport agreements.

Figure B.4 shows there is a relationship between time and cost as consistent trends are evident, although some cases are affected by the difference in national costs of living. This figure shows the high costs of trade transactions in Bangladesh, especially on imports, and Myanmar has particularly high export transaction costs. Sri Lanka has significant import costs, while Bhutan scores well due to the cheap cost of document processing.

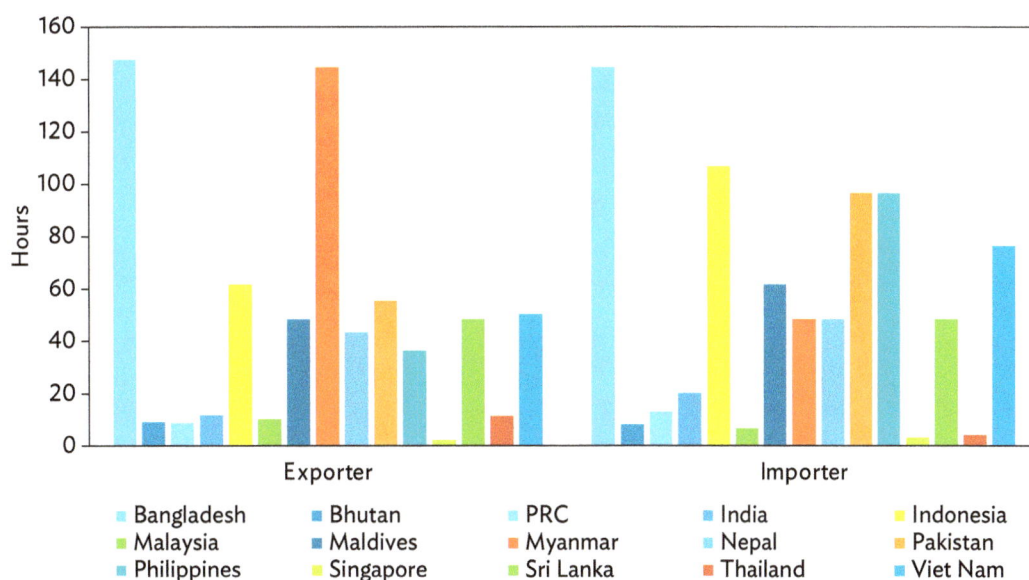

Figure B.3: Time to Comply with Documentary Requirements to Export and Import in Selected Asian Countries, 2020 (hours)

PRC = People's Republic of China.
Source: World Bank. Doing Business Survey.

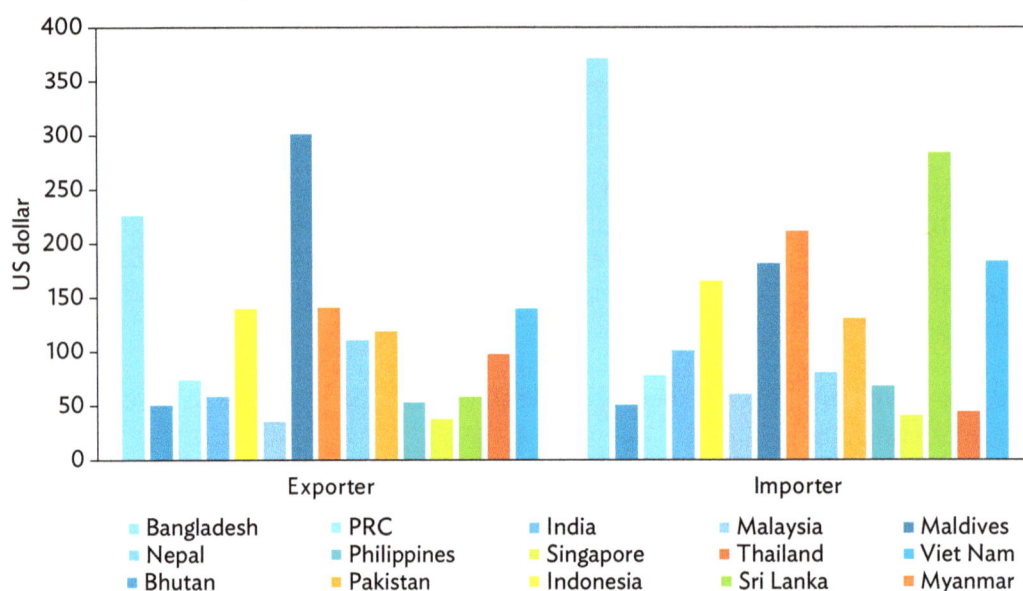

Figure B.4: Cost of Complying with Border Requirements to Export and Import, South Asia Subregional Economic Cooperation and Regional Comparators, 2020

PRC = People's Republic of China.
Source: World Bank. Doing Business.

In August 2020, the World Bank identified irregularities in the compilation of its Doing Business Surveys for the 2018 and the later 2020 surveys, particularly in the methodology applied. At this stage, the irregularities are not thought to be of a scale warranting that their use is invalid, although they should possibly only be considered in addition to other performance indicators rather than in isolation.

Conclusions

International surveys provide a degree of benchmarking comparing the trade facilitation situations in BIMSTEC countries and those in adjacent markets. While they measure different aspects of trade facilitation—from the "narrow" to the "broad" and the "new generation" definitions—there is an element of consistency throughout.

The surveys generally show that Thailand is perceived to have the most advanced trade facilitation conditions in the BIMSTEC region, but still scores lower than Malaysia and Singapore. Thailand is heavily dependent on global value chains and this requires good trade facilitation practices to support these forms of advanced production. India is perceived as having a relatively advanced trade facilitation environment, though behind Thailand's. India is the largest trading country in the BIMSTEC region and is also heavily engaged in global value chains and more advanced logistical activities. Sri Lanka ranks above Bangladesh in most of these surveys. Both counties also participate significantly in GVCs, although not to the same extent as Thailand and India. Bhutan, Myanmar, and Nepal have limited exposure to GVC trade, and the surveys indicate less advanced trade facilitation environments.

The surveys suggest the BIMSTEC Trade Facilitation Strategic Framework 2030 should address these differences between member states to attempt to narrow them. Implementing the TFA measures is an important starting point in progressing toward more advanced processing and procedures. The agreement, however, tends to concentrate on customs, and there is a need for a much wider scope involving the activities of other government border agencies. As the focus moves more toward the "new generation" definition, potential constraints in Bangladesh and Myanmar in particular are noted in the Logistics Performance Index time and cost assessments. The surveys indicate significant improvements when compared with previous survey data, but over time the trade facilitation demands have been further evolving and there is an ongoing need to 'catch up' with the developed countries and those present in neighboring countries, many of whom are trade competitors.

www.ingramcontent.com/pod-product-compliance
Lightning Source LLC
Chambersburg PA
CBHW050044220326
41599CB00045B/7271